KENT
RAILWAYS
David Staines
THE AGE OF STEAM

COUNTRYSIDE BOOKS
NEWBURY BERKSHIRE

First published 2010
© David Staines 2010

COUNTRYSIDE BOOKS
3 Catherine Road
Newbury, Berkshire

To view our complete range of books,
please visit us at
www.countrysidebooks.co.uk

ISBN 978 1 84674 211 8

Designed by Peter Davies, Nautilus Design
Produced through MRM Associates Ltd., Reading
Printed by Information Press, Oxford

Contents

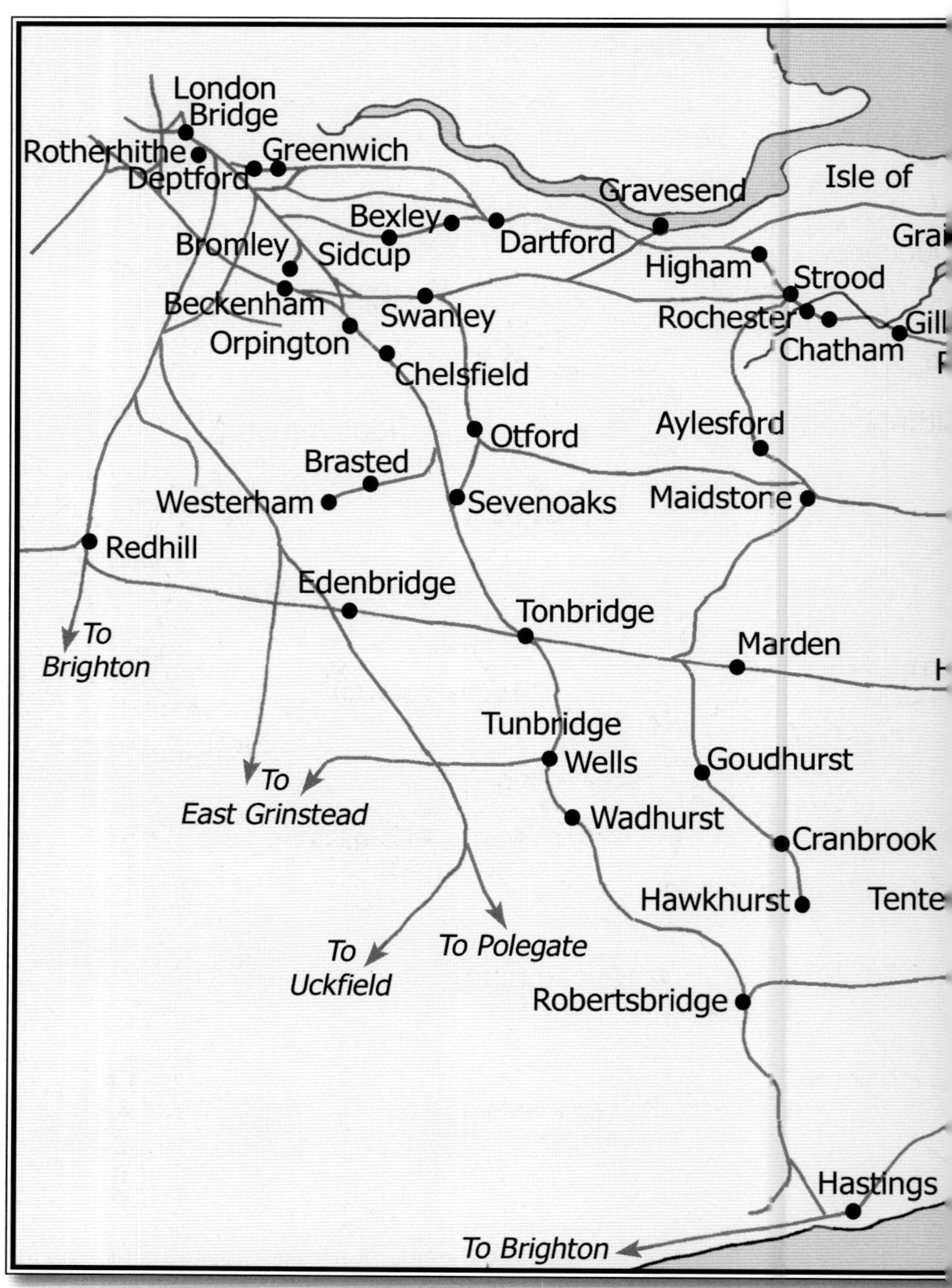

London Bridge
Rotherhithe
Greenwich
Deptford
Gravesend
Isle of
Grai
Bexley
Dartford
Bromley
Sidcup
Higham
Strood
Beckenham
Swanley
Rochester
Gill
Orpington
Chatham
Chelsfield
Aylesford
Otford
Brasted
Westerham
Sevenoaks
Maidstone
Redhill
Edenbridge
Tonbridge
To Brighton
Marden
H
Tunbridge
Wells
Goudhurst
To
East Grinstead
Wadhurst
Cranbrook
Hawkhurst
Tente
To Polegate
To
Uckfield
Robertsbridge
Hastings
To Brighton

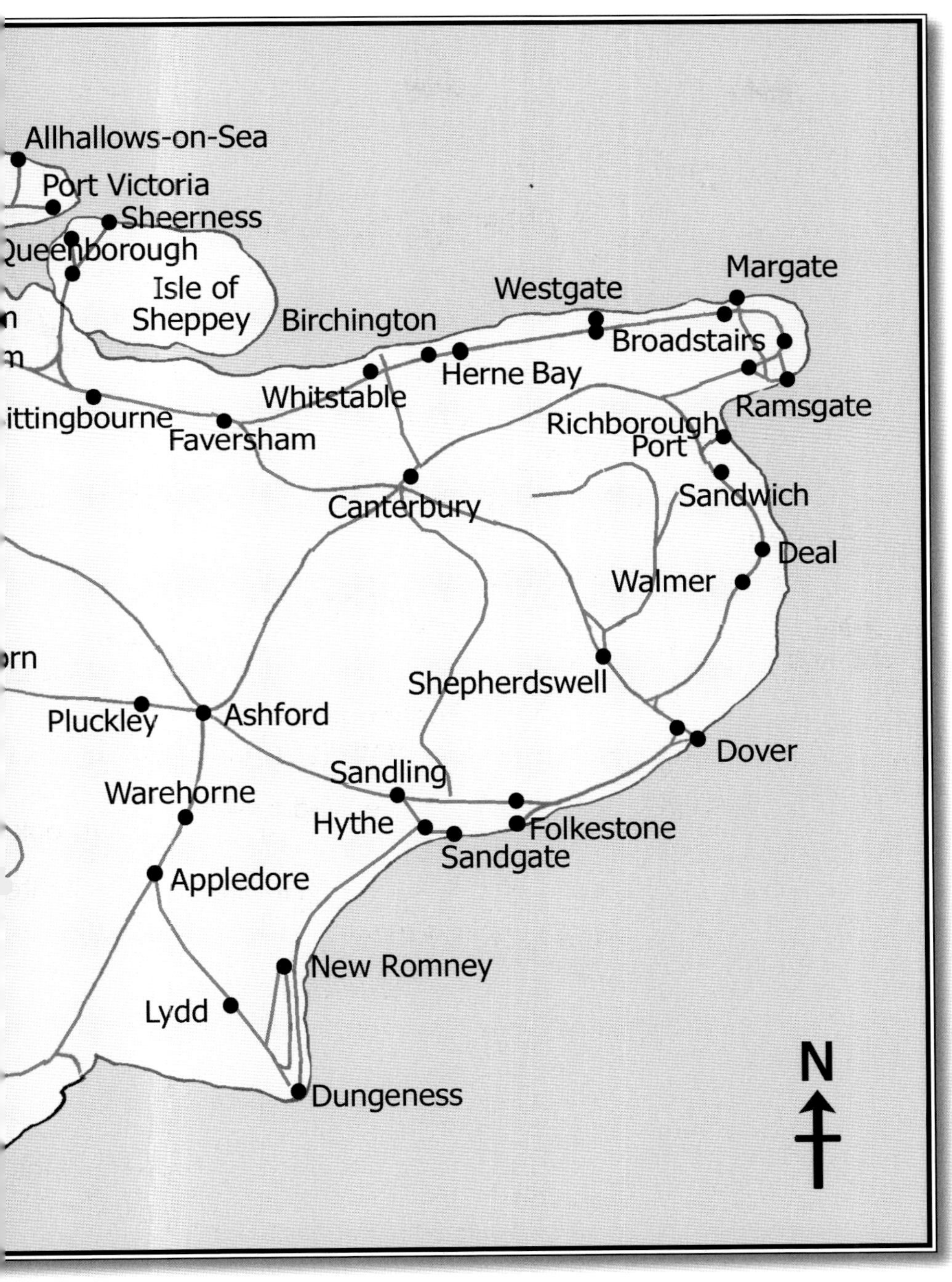

Allhallows-on-Sea
Port Victoria
Sheerness
Queenborough
Isle of Sheppey
Birchington
Westgate
Margate
Broadstairs
Herne Bay
Whitstable
ittingbourne
Faversham
Richborough Port
Ramsgate
Sandwich
Canterbury
Deal
Walmer
Shepherdswell
Pluckley
Ashford
Dover
Sandling
Warehorne
Hythe
Folkestone
Sandgate
Appledore
New Romney
Lydd
Dungeness
N

Introduction

In the history of our island, the county of Kent holds a special place. Its position so close to the Continent saw it at the forefront of commercial travel from the days long before the Romans until air travel finally eclipsed international journeys over land and sea. In the 19th and 20th centuries the railways played the dominant role in the task of moving just about everything from people to goods and, for much of that time, steam was king. The first railways were driven through Kent because of the need to link the capital with firstly the Channel ports and later the county's towns and communities. However, as soon as the tracks were hewn out of the chalk and clay, the railways themselves changed the 'Garden of England' forever. Not just physically, but economically and socially. Kent's railways saw some world firsts; the first commuter railway and the first steam locomotive to haul passengers.

A typical scene of the steam age in Kent. The 2.15 pm boat train from Victoria to Folkestone Harbour passes Headcorn on 27th May 1959. (R.C. Riley)

The steam scene in Kent turns full circle. USA class tank locomotive 30065 Maunsell, *named after one of the Southern Railway's locomotive and carriage designers, was one of the last two steam locomotives operated by British Railways in Kent. In April 2009 it stands in the yard at Tunbridge Wells West on the preserved Spa Valley Railway. (Author)*

In later years, the two major railway companies in the county embarked on the fiercest railway 'turf wars' of the Victorian age. As *The Times* remembered, 'the little overlapping companies were always good for a laugh, sometimes ribald, every now and then sardonic. The London, Chatham and Dover became the Undone, Smash'em and Turn'em Over. The South Eastern mainline was the scene of the fictitious tragedy in which a would-be suicide laid his neck on the line and died of starvation.'

Many volumes have been written about the railways of Kent, from the lines themselves to the locomotives and rolling stock that ran upon them. This book attempts to look on it from a slightly different perspective. The history and development of the system is an inescapable part of the overall story, but that story also encompasses the social effects, economic changes and the opportunities that the railways brought. There are some fascinating accounts explaining why the lines were built where they were, and what effect they had on the development on a whole variety of places. We all know of Dover, Folkestone and Margate, but what of Port Victoria, Dungeness and Allhallows-on-Sea?

Whilst the age of steam is regarded by most people with misty-eyed nostalgia, was it really that good for those who had to contend with it on a daily basis? The reality is that whilst it died a mostly unlamented death, it has been reborn, phoenix-like, into a new existence in the leisure and heritage industry. To this very day, Kent's hundreds of thousands of commuters, whilst no longer pulled by steam, have their journeys influenced by the promoters and builders of the railways of that age, even down to their fundamental decision of where to live.

The story of the age of steam in Kent and how it influenced everyone in the county is a rich one. From London to Dover, from Queen Victoria to the 'first great train robber', from gold and silver to hops and coal, from the 'Golden Arrow' to the trucks carrying horse manure from the capital's streets to enrich the county's crops, this book looks at the age of steam and its legacy from more than a purely mechanical perspective.

David Staines

Acknowledgements

There are always a great number of people who need to be thanked when it comes to acknowledging the part they have played in bringing a volume such as this together. To start with my thanks go to Robin Jones, editor of *Heritage Railway* magazine, who put my name forward to the publishers when this book was first mooted. It is perhaps entirely appropriate that I received the publishers' phone call whilst visiting one of Kent's ancient castles!

No book is complete without its photographs and this book would not have happened without the invaluable assistance of three people in sourcing its steam age pictures. Their help is all the more pertinent in that a few key photographic collections have recently been split up and sold following the passing away of those who had kept them intact for many years. Their custodians had always made them freely available to ventures such as this.

My deepest debt of gratitude is to Rodney Lissenden who researched and made available to me an awe-inspiring selection of pictures from the collection of the late Dick Riley. My thanks also to Dick's widow Christine for allowing me to use them. My heartfelt thanks also go to Chris Milner and Phil Marsh at the *Railway Magazine*. They both allowed me a day to roam unrestricted through the magazine's astounding archive where the photographic distractions were immeasurable.

A final word on the pictures – a side effect of dipping into hitherto relatively untapped photographic sources is that many of the images reproduced here have never been previously published, itself a rarity. Some of the prints reproduced have become a little bit 'careworn' over the years – in some cases the prints are approaching 100 years old. I was faced with a dilemma of whether to digitally enhance parts of them in order to give them a cleaner appearance than their years would otherwise allow. I have decided against on the grounds that I believe most readers of this book would appreciate the character of a picture rather than look at a computer assisted image.

On a more personal note my thanks go to my wife Hilary for a large chunk of word processing and my daughter Katie for the joint photographic expeditions we have been on. Keeping it in the family, my thanks also go to my father for proof reading the text. If he had not introduced me to an Adams O2 in the dying years of Southern Region steam, perhaps this book might never have been written …

One of the most significant achievements of the steam preservation era was the completion in 2009 of the brand new 4-6-2 LNER design locomotive 'Tornado'. The locomotive has since made many forays into Kent and is here seen setting out on the racing straight from Tonbridge towards Ashford with an excursion bound for Canterbury. (Author)

1

EARLY DAYS

The strategic importance of the county of Kent today is very different from that of 150 years ago. Today, most people think of the county as a patchwork of mostly pleasant towns and villages, with London exerting a heavy commuter influence on the 'Garden of England'. In the story of the county, this is a recent change. For most of the last thousand years, Kent has been both the gateway to the Continent and bastion against invasion. For this reason it held a unique importance in the United Kingdom and, together with fortification, transport links between the capital and the English Channel have been of paramount importance since the time of the Romans.

After a couple of false starts, the Romans invaded in AD 43 and set up their first military and commercial stronghold at Richborough near Sandwich. The first and most important Roman road in the country was driven across Kent to the developing capital of London. It became the busiest commercial and military highway in the land – the 'old' A2 road follows most of its course to this day. Within a short while, Dover usurped Richborough as the principal port. The strategic overland flow of traffic was to remain a key goal for the builders of the railways 1,800 years after the Romans passed.

TWO PIONEERS

Curiously, the first railway in Kent came about as a result of much more domestic concerns. The cathedral city of Canterbury, as well as being the seat of the church, was an important commercial centre. By the 1820s the local worthies were becoming increasingly frustrated by the silting up of the River Stour, the principal means of conveying heavy goods in and out via the sea. In Cornwall and the North East, wagon ways, together with locomotive propulsion, had become established as the cutting edge of transport technology. Inspired by this, George Stephenson engineered a 6-mile railway from the city to Whitstable on the North Kent coast. Whitstable was a sleepy fishing village where a new harbour would be built, which would become Canterbury's new port. The railway opened in 1830 and was provided with just one locomotive, *Invicta*, a product of Stephenson's works at Gateshead on the River

Tyne. Kent's first railway was in business, although in reality it was a false dawn. The isolated line had severe gradients and it spent a decade being worked by stationary winding engines until locomotive technology developed sufficiently to cope with its challenges. It saw its last train in 1953 and, apart from the harbour at Whitstable and a tunnel beneath Tyler Hill, very little of it is visible today.

A more significant development was taking place at the other end of the county. That Greenwich (now an inner London borough) should be considered part of the story of railways in Kent seems curious now, but in the early 19th century it was totally divorced from the capital, a place of naval, scientific and fashionable significance. It was the first stop on the Dover road reached by either the River Thames or stagecoach past the meadows and market gardens of Bermondsey and Rotherhithe. This line was only 3¾ miles long, yet its promoters had Dover well and truly in their sights. It was engineered by a military man, Colonel G.T. Landmann, who projected his line entirely on a brick viaduct in order to avoid low marshy ground and to cross various streets on the final approach to London. When the first section from Spa Road, Bermondsey to Deptford opened in February 1836, it became the first suburban railway in the world and on completion London Bridge became the

The opening day of the Canterbury & Whitstable Railway on 3rd May 1830, showing one of the first trains dropping down towards the city. Canterbury Cathedral dominates the skyline whilst admiring crowds line the route. (National Railway Museum/ Science and Society Picture Library)

On the Canterbury & Whitstable Railway, Invicta hauls a loaded train away from Whitstable Harbour. A view of the opening day as recorded from Church Street, with the Isle of Sheppey in the background. (National Railway Museum/ Science and Society Picture Library)

first capital city terminus in the world. In many ways, it reflected the railway of 21st-century Kent. Firstly, and against the grain of most other railways built in that era, it operated frequent trains, usually every 15–20 minutes, and conveyed passengers only. No goods or freight were carried. With the railway connecting two established sources of traffic, its arrival was not a stimulus for a great deal of speculative building although the relentless expansion of London obliterated the rustic nature of the journey soon after the line opened. Like all pioneering enterprises, it adopted various practices which, following experience, were abandoned and now seemed quaint or unusual. For some years, at night the entire 3¾ mile viaduct was lit by gaslight. At its three permanent stations, London Bridge, Deptford and Greenwich, inclined planes were built, dropping from the viaduct down to ground level. It was thought that gentlemen's carriages could be driven up from the street and conveyed upon wagons on the railway. That this was a fairly pointless exercise for such a short railway and that none were actually carried is a clear pointer to the aspirations of the railway to longer distance travel. However, before long, gentlemen were leaving

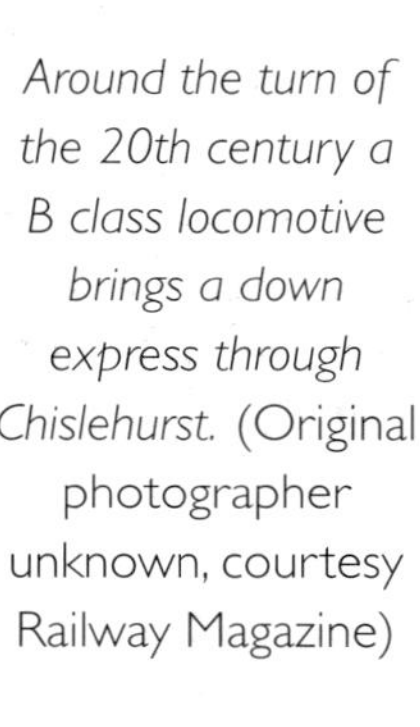

Around the turn of the 20th century a B class locomotive brings a down express through Chislehurst. (Original photographer unknown, courtesy Railway Magazine)

their horses at stables provided beneath the viaduct and continuing to their city job by train. 'Park and ride' and the social phenomenon of suburbia were born. Despite setting so many portents for the future, the London & Greenwich never expanded any further. Having reaped the benefits of leisure travel to Greenwich Park, the railway's desire to extend further and ultimately to Dover would have bisected the park to the objection of both the Admiralty and the Royal Observatory. The Admiralty was unmoved by the offer of a graceful viaduct with niches for the display of busts of naval heroes 'past, present and future'. The Astronomer Royal was similarly unimpressed by a suggested concession allowing him to order the stopping of trains if they interfered with his experiments. Greenwich remained a terminus for many years. Another way would have to be found for the railway to conquer Kent and reach Dover.

DOVER

Final peace with France following the end of the Napoleonic Wars saw even greater leaps in commerce. There was also premium traffic to and from the Empire. Here, speed was of the essence for a heady mix of passengers and cargo, from royalty and

An up Dover–London boat train passes beneath the white cliffs on the approach to Shakespeare Tunnel hauled by 'Lord Nelson' class locomotive No 856 in Southern Railway days. (Dr Ian C. Allen, R.C. Riley collection)

diplomats to mail and gold bullion. Valuable time could be saved by replacing the last sea leg of the journey from the English Channel up the Thames to a (relatively) fast transit by rail.

There was an assortment of schemes to link various parts of the county, and the eminent engineer Thomas Telford proposed a line close to Watling Street serving Gravesend, Chatham and Canterbury. However, some backers preferred to engineer a more straightforward line, which would avoid the necessity of crossing the Medway and cutting through the higher parts of the North Downs. Their preferred route took advantage of an almost flat run from Edenbridge to within a few miles of Folkestone. It was this line that became the genesis of the South Eastern Railway and was authorised by Parliament in 1836. This group of influential Victorian industrialists included many investors from the north of England. It is a quirk of fate that some of the meetings that had a profound effect on Kent actually took place in Manchester. It was no coincidence that the Liverpool & Manchester Railway, the world's first 'intercity' railway, had opened in 1830 and in the early days the officers of the South Eastern Railway frequently turned to Manchester for advice on a whole variety of issues.

The advantages of the flat, straight run for nearly 50 miles across the Vale of Kent were apparent for all to see. It was at either end that complications arose. Popular history has it that the SER was forced into a roundabout route out of London that involved sharing tracks with three other railway companies solely at the insistence of Parliament. The London & Greenwich, London & Croydon and the Brighton railways all shared the same line out of the capital. Parliament insisted only one railway line would be needed from the capital towards the south and east. Therefore the line to Dover was also subject to this principle. Accordingly, it was only permitted to strike out eastwards to the Kent coast from a junction at a remote spot south of Croydon, now known as Redhill. Whilst this was an inconvenient and circuitous route, it had the advantage of being substantially cheaper than having to forge a new route out of London and through the North Downs (something the SER was forced to do in later years). Building this first railway saw the SER becoming increasingly short of funds whilst it still had to spend large sums of money at the other end of the line. The last stretch between Folkestone and Dover was spectacularly hewn out of the famous white cliffs. The line was carried on a ledge with the sea cliffs being variously cut through, tunnelled through or blasted clean out of the way.

The South Eastern was so eager to grab the Continental traffic at the earliest opportunity that before the engineering work beyond Folkestone was finished, it bought the town's harbour. This had been built by Thomas Telford in 1809 for the sum of £69,000 but had already fallen on hard times and had become prone to silting up. The SER snapped it up for a bargain £18,000 and immediately started

A South Eastern & Chatham Railway D class waits by Margate shed. Note the graceful lines of a classic Victorian locomotive. (Original photographer unknown, courtesy Railway Magazine)

international traffic via Folkestone. It must have been a ghastly business as passengers were transported by road from a temporary station a mile from the harbour and at low tide would have to be rowed out to the waiting Channel packets. It is little wonder that the SER was desperate to reach the deepwater port of Dover. In due course cross Channel traffic was handled from both ports, Folkestone's harbour becoming greatly improved over the following 100 years.

By 1844 the line was complete and the goal achieved. The UK leg of the London to Paris run could be accomplished by rail at the astounding average speed of 30 mph. It would be some time before rails connected Paris with the French coast on the other side of the Channel. Although the railway's financial affairs were reflected by the meanness of its first stations (which were mostly simple wooden structures) the main line itself was well laid out, the long straight 'racing stretch' being punctuated by passing loops at a few strategic intervals. There was further expansion in the air when Tunbridge Wells was reached by a branch from Tonbridge, which opened in 1845. A branch from Ashford up the valley of the River Stour gave Canterbury a main line service, the line continuing on to Margate Sands, opening in 1846. For an early railway the South Eastern established a fairly good reputation. Like the 'Garden of England' it served, everything looked rosy. However, it was a short-lived honeymoon because, for the rest of its existence, it was racked by turbulence and commercial warfare. And it only had itself to blame.

The South Eastern now looked to further expansion, particularly in the North Kent area. Unable to get past Greenwich Park, a completely new line was built, opening in 1849 from a junction midway between London Bridge and Greenwich, which then headed off through Woolwich and Dartford to Gravesend. Here it met the Thames and Medway navigation canal. The canal had cut a course between Gravesend and Strood, allowing shipping to avoid a detour around the Isle of Grain when sailing between London and the Medway towns. The canal company had already converted their operation by laying a single railway line on the towpath and this had included the passage through two substantial tunnels between Higham and Strood. The South Eastern bought out the canal company and laid a new double track main line adjacent to the canal. Inside the tunnels the canal was drained and the railway built on top. At Strood the canal basin was retained for the transfer of waterborne traffic. Now, the SER proudly boasted a link from London to Rochester and Chatham, conveniently forgetting that the line ended at Strood on the opposite side of the Medway from Rochester and still a further two miles from Chatham. Further along the coast, sizeable towns such as Sittingbourne and Faversham had even less.

AN INTERLOPER STOKES THE FIRES

All that these towns had were just vague promises and assertions from the South Eastern's directors that the railway would come to them in due course. The worthies and landowners of these towns soon concluded that in reality nothing was happening. Fed up with empty promises, they promoted their own line, the 'East Kent Railway', which linked Strood, the centre of Chatham and the North Kent towns with Canterbury. This coincided with a period of infighting within the SER board and mistrust between the board and their shareholders. The internal situation had become so bad that the shareholders had forced the board into a policy requiring shareholder approval for any major project. At the time, the board had been squandering money supporting other weaker railways in a bid to gain extra traffic. That the whole situation had degenerated during a period of financial downturn only added to the incapacity of the directors, who then became divided as to whether an expansionist policy was appropriate.

This was the climate in which others saw more potential in the East Kent Railway than just a line linking a few towns together. Although initially only built as a single line, the East Kent's promoters were quite happy to hide behind an accepted façade that they were only extending the South Eastern's line to Strood for the benefit of towns the SER were unable to serve. No doubt the SER thought the minnow would perish and could be bought up in due course at a give-away price saving it the bother

Edward Watkin's headquarters, the offices of the South Eastern Railway at London Bridge station. (Author)

of building the line in the first place. It even undertook to allow the East Kent's trains into Strood station and not to object to an extension from Canterbury to Dover. The East Kent then played its trump card. The SER, sensing things were now getting out of hand, refused the newcomer access to the line between Strood and Dartford. The East Kent simply obtained Parliamentary power for a new direct line from Strood to St Mary Cray where a further company had already obtained permission to link St Mary Cray with Bromley (now Shortlands), which itself was at the end of a branch line served from London Victoria. In bits and pieces, what had started as a backwater landowner's railway had now created a through London–Dover railway in total opposition to the South Eastern. In 1859 the 'East Kent' formally changed its name to the 'London, Chatham & Dover Railway'. The 'Chatham' opened to Dover in 1861 and the stage was set for a bloody battle between the two railways, which forged the shape of the railway network in Kent to this day.

The fires of competition between the SER and the LC&DR were hot enough at times but were stoked to a white heat by the personalities of the two men who led their respective companies for the next quarter century. History has portrayed the South Eastern's Sir Edward Watkin as a bombastic, stern railway baron in comparison to the Chatham's James Staats Forbes' role as the suave cunning fox. In reality, these are generalisations, but in many ways the men were poles apart. They did share a bizarre desire to get one over on each other and were lifelong protagonists, yet at the same time the reality that cooperation had to be the better option must have been inescapable, although it was usually ignored. The result of this titanic clash was ruthless promotion of financially crippling lines in competition to each other. Throughout Kent, railways were built and promoted by one company, not for the good of the county or as a service to its population, but merely in attempts to snatch traffic away from the other. With both companies' energies and resources channelled into this disastrous feud, it was the ordinary railway user who suffered on a system starved of any logical investment.

For the next quarter century, the giants slugged it out. The 'Chatham' went to Sheerness and introduced cross Channel sailings from a pier at nearby Queenborough.

On the London, Chatham & Dover Railway the branch to Gravesend West was an example of wasteful competition in building duplicate branch lines. On 11th April 1953 the 4.45 pm Gravesend West–Farningham Road passes the closed station at Rosherville. This once saw buoyant trade as Victorian visitors flocked to nearby pleasure gardens in the days when Gravesend was a fashionable resort. (R.C. Riley)

So the South Eastern built a line across the Isle of Grain and built a new 'port' (in reality just a pier) on the other side of the Medway estuary facing Queenborough to steal the traffic. A Chatham sponsored company built a branch to Sevenoaks, but the SER stole most of the traffic when in 1868 it opened a more direct line for Dover traffic from London to Tonbridge. This line was, however, a much needed shortcut, reducing the journey to the Channel by 22 miles and alleviating the complications of line sharing between London and Redhill, which had reached epidemic proportions. The SER had already extended from Strood to the county town of Maidstone so the Chatham built its own line to Maidstone from the Sevenoaks branch at Otford and then extended it to Ashford where it built its own station striking deep into SER territory. The SER then built a parallel branch across the River Medway from Strood to Chatham, virtually alongside its competitor. It called the terminus 'Chatham Central' although in reality it was anything but central. The South Eastern struck across the Romney Marsh to Dungeness, one of the most isolated spots in the county, on the grounds that a new harbour there might be a good idea. The Chatham, having served Herne Bay on the way to Margate, then decided to carry on to Ramsgate to steal a share of the South Eastern's traffic there. In the process, it managed to mop up the entire holiday trade that was to develop along the North Thanet coastline.

In this litany of wasteful competition, the biggest rows were saved for the cross Channel traffic, to be covered in a subsequent chapter (see pages 52-55, chapter 3), whilst some of the losers were small towns hoping for a branch line. If their citizens didn't happen to be in a position of potential strategic advantage in the overall competition, the chance of one of the big companies coming to their aid and serving their community was slim. It was only after Watkin and Forbes had left the scene that the two companies finally agreed to work together under the title of the South Eastern & Chatham Railway, from 1st January 1899. Legally the two companies remained separate entities.

THE COLONEL'S RAILWAYS

The lines to Hawkhurst, Tenterden and the Kent coalfield bring another character onto the stage of Kent's railways. Holman F. Stephens was a legendary engineer and promoter of railway lines. However, his empire was a very different one from that of Watkin or Forbes. Stephens' first major appointment was as a 22 year old resident engineer on the building of the 11½ mile branch from Paddock Wood to Hawkhurst. Promoted by local interests (the company's seal was appropriately a bunch of hops), permission to build the line as far as the Wealden trading centre of Cranbrook was obtained in 1877. Construction started two years later but ground to a halt due to an inability to raise the appropriate amount of cash. It was not until 1892 that Goudhurst was reached, with the line opening throughout to Hawkhurst

A rare view at Rolvenden on the Kent & East Sussex Railway of both of the line's original locomotives, No 1 Tenterden and No 2 Northiam, flanking one of Colonel Stephens' infamous rail buses in April 1932. (Dr Ian C. Allen, R.C. Riley collection)

in 1893. The line featured economically built stations, sharp gradients and many level crossings, all of which were to become hallmarks of Stephens' future projects. Another recurring feature was the building of stations some distance from the communities they purported to serve, notably Cranbrook and Hawkhurst. Stephens' career was accelerated by the passing of the Light Railways Act of 1896. Parliament had become concerned that rigid regulations stipulating minimum standards for railway infrastructure were frustrating attempts at linking smaller communities to the railway network and stifling their economic development. It sanctioned the building of 'Light Railways' where regulations were more lax on matters such as weight limits and fencing – meaning that only smaller, lighter trains could run and then only at reduced speed limits. This area became Stephens' specialisation and he was appointed engineer and manager of a variety of such railways throughout

A bucolic view of one of the 'Terrier' locomotives forever associated with the Kent & East Sussex Railway. On hire from the Southern Railway, No 2678 is seen at Robertsbridge. Whether the barrel in the foreground held water or beer is a matter of conjecture. Another rare view in that it was taken in wartime on 25th April 1940. (John L. Smith, courtesy Railway Magazine)

the country, either proposed or actually built. Some of the existing more moribund outposts of the railway system also came under his wing.

Whilst Watkin and Forbes ran their empires from grand London chambers, Stephens' centre of operation was more fitting to his aspirations, a tiny office squeezed in between two shops at Quarry Road in Tonbridge. Stephens later gained the title 'Lieutenant Colonel' during the First World War, forever after being referred to as 'Colonel Stephens'. Railway historian A.R. Catt summarised a visit to one of the Colonel's railways thus: 'It was an experience never to be forgotten. One was faced with lines stocked with a bewildering assortment of ancient locomotives and rolling stock. Enthusiasts sometimes had difficulty in identifying the locomotives; one apparently doomed and laid aside on one railway would suddenly appear on another with a new coat of paint. Another difficulty in the identity of individual engines was the fact that the Colonel had marked preferences for certain mythological names which he applied to successive engines on the same line, or to different contemporary locomotives on another line. An example was the name "Hesperus" which cropped up on at least three of the lines, and another "Hecate" on two.'

The railway that became the epitome of Stephens' motley empire was the Kent & East Sussex. In the middle of the Weald the town of Tenterden, once a limb of the famous Cinque Ports and still a thriving centre of trade, had been left off the railway map for the simple reason that it wasn't on the route to anywhere else more profitable. Local promoters took advantage of the Light Railway Act as a chance to tap into that revenue and link the town to Robertsbridge on the main line to Hastings, picking up some more rural trade on the way. The railway was opened, using the short-lived title of the Rother Valley Railway, from Robertsbridge to an initial terminus at Tenterden (the station is now Rolvenden) in 1900. Within three years there had been further expansion to Tenterden Town and later through to Headcorn on the Tonbridge–Ashford main line, together with a change of name to the Kent & East Sussex Railway. Two brand new locomotives and six carriages had been bought when the railway first opened, and these were the only new rolling stock the line ever saw. Thereafter it relied on second, third and fourth hand locomotives and carriages from other railways, most of which when expired took up residence in Rolvenden's garden of railway remembrance where they would gently moulder away into the undergrowth. The K&ESR was particularly averse to scrapping old rolling stock, partly because everything remained on the books as un-depreciated capital assets and partly because of another feature of the Colonel's railways, that of using the parts of assorted locomotives to make one good enough to return to service. Stephens may have regretted his decision not to allow the K&ESR to be absorbed, like the South Eastern & Chatham Railway, into the Southern Railway upon grouping in 1923 as the 20s saw the railway fall on increasingly hard times. One of the Colonel's most bizarre cost-cutting exercises was the introduction of road motor omnibuses converted to run on rails. A variety of these contraptions were used, pairs of buses running 'back to back' with one towing its partner depending upon the direction of travel. Apart from changing the wheels, little other conversion work was carried out: some even retained their useless steering wheels! The railway thus maintained a highly individualistic life until it finally became part of British Railways in 1948.

Another of the Colonel's independent concerns was the East Kent Light Railway, primarily driven by the development of the Kent coalfield, which we shall look at later. The South Eastern did build a secondary line from Canterbury to Folkestone, serving the scattered communities between the two, and also a branch from

Sandling to Hythe and Sandgate, although the latter was more influenced by an attempt to reach the harbour at Folkestone by a more operationally convenient route. With the exception of the lines around the Kent coalfield, by the close of the 19th century the railway map of Kent was complete – but what a transformation had been wrought upon the county.

On the Kent & East Sussex Railway class O1 31370 waits at Headcorn with a single carriage on 27th July 1953. Only the K&ESR side of the station was known as Headcorn Junction, for the main line side 'Headcorn' sufficed with no suffix. (R.C. Riley)

CHANGING THE COUNTY

Before the coming of the railway transformed the lives of those around it, it first physically changed the landscape of the county itself. The first signs of the impending railway were innocuous enough. Gentlemen on horseback with a small entourage would appear in the most unlikely places, surveying the route. Behind the scenes, promoters and investors would be beavering away whilst, in far away Westminster, Parliament would debate and sometimes give permission for the passage of the railway. Then all hell would be let loose – vast numbers of men together with the most up to date machinery of the age would descend upon sleepy communities who had never seen the like of it before. Although these rural towns and villages might have some idea of what they thought might happen, often their population just didn't know what had hit them. Building the railways was labour intensive in the extreme throughout the Victorian period. The workforce was the 'navvies' or 'navigators'. The name came from the generation before, where on a much smaller scale they had driven (or navigated) the canals through much of the country. A common perception of the navvies is that they were itinerant and frequently hailed from Ireland. Many were, but just as many were local agricultural labourers driven off the land by increasing mechanisation together with the lure of a 'quick buck' – although in reality the 'buck' wasn't that 'quick'. Frequently workers were paid partly by ticket or token that could only be redeemed for food, essentials and alcohol in the railway contractor's own shops. This practice, known as the truck system, was subsequently outlawed. The popular image of the navvies is a hard working, hard drinking, marauding crime wave that passed through the landscape. The railway contractors appointed their own constables in an attempt to keep order although this was not always successful. At Christmas 1841 the navvies were reported as having rioted and injured those charged with keeping the peace. Attempts were made to satisfy the men's religious needs and, accordingly, tin chapels would be set up as the

*An example of the impact that the navvies (or 'miners')
had on local communities is the retention of the name
on a pub at Dunton Green in the 21st century. Both
Polhill and Sevenoaks tunnels were nearby, perhaps giving
an explanation as to why this particular name was used.*
(Katie Staines)

work progressed to allow them to attend Sunday services without terrifying the gentry at the local parish church. Petty crime and hard drinking were rife, with many communities duly scandalised. Although there was early earth moving machinery available, most of the work was back breaking and life threatening. Five men died pushing the line beyond Folkestone through the cliffs to Dover, whilst fatalities resulting from what would now be called industrial injuries were rife.

A NEW LEGACY

Apart from a traumatised community, what did the navvies leave behind? The landscape was changed forever. Today we see graceful Victorian viaducts enhancing the landscape; however, the railway has had over a century to mellow and during construction and soon after was seen as a brutalist blot on the landscape. It really didn't matter in what manner the railway was cut through the environment, the most effective way to engineer the project usually prevailed. Railways by their nature need wide curves and easy gradients, but where the landscape was unyielding the line was usually driven straight through it. With chalk being so common throughout the county, many embankments were initially a dazzling white. Chalk excavated from the tunnels through the North Downs was used to build the high embankment between Chelsfield and Orpington, which was said to have been a notorious white eyesore visible from miles around. As noted before, Round Down Cliff, between Folkestone and Dover, was simply blown away with explosives.

Occasionally, the structures on the early lines gained early aesthetic appeal. The

The viaduct at Eynsford has become a local landmark and is a visual legacy of Victorian railway engineering. Structures such as this were once deemed an eyesore but now complement their environment. A 'Schools' class crosses in March 1948. (British Railways Southern Region, courtesy Railway Magazine)

long viaduct between London Bridge and Greenwich actually attracted a following, although as the century progressed the general design and ornamentation of bridges, viaducts and tunnels steadily declined. Of course, if you were wealthy enough you could afford to avoid the railway spoiling your environment. If you were the local landowner you could simply refuse to sell the railway any land and it would have to go elsewhere. Alternatively, you could select which part of your plot you would sell and manipulate the situation to your advantage, perhaps by demanding that a station be built in a nearby location with the right to have trains stopped for your personal use. The owner of Sandling Park outside Folkestone safeguarded the view from his drawing room by inserting a clause, on selling his land, providing for a short tunnel to be built for no other purpose. Incidentally, this requirement returned to haunt the builders of the Channel Tunnel Rail Link when they had to construct a parallel tunnel for the 186 mph Eurostar operation over 150 years later! With Kent being a primarily agricultural county, when the railways arrived there was little wholesale cutting through of slums or communities to make way for the tracks, although this did feature around the Medway towns. Whilst today we celebrate our architectural and industrial heritage, the Victorian engineers had no such concerns. When building the line from Minster to Deal, the SER sliced through the ancient remains of the old harbour area adjacent to the fort at Richborough, the first gateway to the county, whilst at Orpington most of the remains of a great Roman house were swept away to make room for sidings.

Although some may have bemoaned the aesthetic change to the county's appearance, for the vast majority a new railway was welcomed with open arms. Once towns and villages learned that a route was being projected in their direction, there would be immediate petitions for wayside stations. And when the railway came, its effects would be utterly unprecedented. Over 150 years ago the steam train was the cutting edge of technology. People who had only managed to travel as far and as fast as a horse could take them were now able to move freely around the county, and even travel to London. The railway brought a telegraph with it. For the first time it was possible for villagers to communicate along wires with the outside world. Mail, goods and supplies could be brought in and local produce could be taken away from the towns and villages of Kent within hours instead of days and weeks. For example the road from London to Tunbridge Wells was one of the best in the country yet the journey took all day by stagecoach, from dawn until dusk, stopping off at inns to change horses on the way. In the 1830s the best possible time was four hours in what was known as a 'fast fly'. When the railways came, one age passed and another arrived. Within a few years Tunbridge Wells had two main line stations operated by different competing companies, with journey times to London down to just over an hour. Towns such as Tonbridge and Ashford, well served by railways, grew. Those off the railway or even on the periphery of key routes such as Sandwich and Westerham remained stable or even declined.

THE COASTAL RESORTS

The resorts around the Thanet coastline from Herne Bay to Ramsgate all owe their development to the railway in some shape or form as each developed in subtly different ways. Before the coming of the railway Margate and Ramsgate were already catering for the tourist trade. By the mid 18th century Margate was welcoming the middle and upper class visitor to its assembly rooms, bathing machines and facilities for 'taking the seawater'. When Ramsgate's fortunes as a port declined it jumped on the same bandwagon and picked up a trade in visitors, albeit more limited. Most of those who came had to be hardy enough to endure an uncertain trip from London by sailing vessel, which would take all day or longer, frequently in a converted cargo 'hoy'. The really wealthy could take the stagecoach to Canterbury and make their own way forward to the coast from there, a process that would also take all day. In the years before the arrival of the railways it was the replacement of sail by steamships that caused the advent of the day-tripper and the spur for Ramsgate and particularly Margate to take off as resorts for the masses. This in turn stimulated development at Herne Bay although there was not a great deal of interest here initially – its new pier being mostly used by steamboat passengers travelling on to Canterbury and Dover by road.

The arrival of the London, Chatham & Dover Railway changed everything. The 'masses' could now easily reach Margate for a day out. The town had preserved its gentility on the basis that only the upper classes could afford the sea trip, the rigours of which ensured that even the hardiest would stay a while before venturing back. With the ease by which the railway could now convey all and sundry, the LC&DR turned Margate into a working class resort almost overnight. A contemporary account reveals: 'On arrival of a cheap excursionist train, those who come by it have their attention very much divided between the sea view and where to get something to eat … the supreme delight with which working-men and their wives and children walk nearly up to their knees in salt water … must be seen to be believed. A hearty meal on arrival, some three or four hours spent walking barefoot on the sands and in the salt water, another repast similar to the first … and then back to the railway station. The excursionists go to the seaside to enjoy themselves after their own fashion. They may be occasionally a little rough in their language, but they mean no harm and the railway officials all bear testimony to the order and regularity they observe on the trip, both to and from their destination.' The town's previous upper and middle class clientele remained none the less offended and looked elsewhere, finding solace in the establishment of smaller; more select resorts such as nearby Westgate, Birchington and Broadstairs, all of which grew up from negligible beginnings. They developed on a more sedate scale and, although also served by the 'Chatham' on the same line to Margate, they have retained a more refined air to this day.

Curiously enough the coming of the railway did not kill off the steamboat trade completely, with some trippers enjoying the novelty of what had become a more civilised and reliable waterborne trip in one direction and using the train in the other. In the same way that the railway changed Margate it also changed Herne Bay's fortunes. Being the nearest of the Thanet seaside resorts to London, the journey was slightly shorter yet it managed to attract a mix of all comers and in due course became a 'middle of the road' place to visit, embracing all and being offended by none.

SOUTHERN
1256

A view of Ramsgate in Southern Railway days. C class 1256 departs with a Margate–Ashford stopping train. (Rev A.W.V. Mace, R.C. Riley collection)

Whilst the Thanet resorts are still today thought of as leisure destinations, Folkestone does not so immediately come to mind, yet for a short period it shot to a peak of fashionableness only to disappear again just as quickly. Again it would not have been possible without the railway. Before the South Eastern arrived it was just a fishing village. Eager to grab the Continental traffic, the SER had bought the moribund harbour and introduced a cross Channel shipping service. Allied to this the company built the town's first hotel and in due course 'society' followed, not just to pass through but to stay. In the same way that many European resorts today concentrate on encouraging a particular type of clientele, so it was with Folkestone. Through the Radnor Estates, local landowner Lord Radnor promoted new hotels that concentrated exclusively on the top end of the market. Fashionable people luxuriated in grand cliff top hotels, all set in their own grounds, with the Metropole the grandest of them all. Funicular lifts took guests down to the beach. This was where the wealthiest families and their domestic entourage could be whisked by the South Eastern's fastest trains. Without the railway serving the town, such development would have been impossible and before long the wealthy tourist traffic was so important that the SER was operating bespoke Pullman services to Folkestone for the leisure market. This became completely independent from passengers being conveyed to the harbour for the Continent. The dramatic change to the social fabric of the country after the First World War brought a sudden end to the town's brief but glorious years as an upmarket resort.

THE RESORT THAT NEVER WAS

With the proven success of the 19th-century railway stimulating existing resorts, in the 1930s the Southern Railway (in conjunction with the Kent and London County Councils) decided to give the concept another airing. However, between them they should have heeded the proverbial warning of putting the cart before the horse. Twinkling over the Thames estuary the Southern Railway saw the lights of the honey pot of Southend and hit on the idea that what Essex could do across the water, Kent would not just match but could vastly exceed. All it needed was a bit of stimulation. Why not buy a large amount of speculative land on the coast in the middle of nowhere right opposite Southend, build a railway to it and sit back and wait for the inevitable visitors to arrive in order to establish a buzzing brand new resort? The largest swimming pool in the UK was planned with the first artificial wave generator in Europe, together with an amusement park four times the size of its nearest contemporary at Blackpool. The Southern duly built the railway and sat back and waited … and waited. Allhallows-on-Sea, the ghostly resort that never was, was born.

In August 1931 a short 1¾ mile branch line was built from a junction at Middle Stoke on the existing Isle of Grain branch to a terminus at a remote spot near Avery

Farm where the Allhallows-on-Sea Estate Company was entrusted with the task of not only developing the holiday resort but also stimulating residential growth as well. As soon as the line was opened two through commuter trains were laid on to Charing Cross every day, but nobody used them as there were no houses to live in. The *Southern Railway Magazine* trumpeted: 'Near the small village of Allhallows, amid fields where cattle graze and the ploughman walks his furrow, workmen are busy constructing roads and laying the main drains and conduits for the gas, water, telephone and electric light services to houses of which not a brick has yet been laid. In contrast to the urban development of an earlier year, the prospective house purchaser and season ticket holder at Allhallows will approach his future home from a modern reinforced concrete carriageway, instead of stumbling through the ruts of an unmade road.' In reality the workmen had replaced the cattle, and ploughmen walking their furrows were pretty thin on the ground in the first place. No season ticket was ever sold and not a single residential brick was ever laid. The station was suitably set back from the 'beach' in order not to prejudice the inevitable growth that it was thought would spring up as the resort took off. But nothing else was ever built except a solitary art deco style block of flats next to the station, a large pub and a short length of promenade by the shoreline. Roads were laid out which went nowhere, and still do so to this day. The line did, however, attract day-trippers. Excursions were laid on, and on Sundays in the 1930s thousands did come to visit but found little to do. The only attraction was the 'seaside' proximity to south-east

The lonely platform at Allhallows-on-Sea as H class 31308 waits to depart for Gravesend on 28th October 1961. The Pilot pub stands in isolation behind the station.
(V. Sellar, courtesy Railway Magazine)

London and west Kent. Nobody stayed the night. Sunday school day trips from Dartford and Deptford were not what the SR had in mind. The railway failed in its task and finally closed in 1961. Ironically, today, Allhallows has become a 'resort' of sorts; most of the area is covered by caravan parks, a fate shared by the site of the station where the water tower used to replenish steam locomotives still survives in the middle of it. Today the flats, known as 'Albany Court', and the pub, the Pilot, still survive as a stark memorial to the railway resort that never was.

SUBURBIA – THE ULTIMATE TRANSFORMATION

It was in the north and west of the county that the railway had its most far reaching effect. In 1836 the London & Greenwich crossed fields and meadows within a few hundred yards of leaving London Bridge. As late as 1857 Dickens described reaching the countryside at New Cross. The railway was stimulating urban development yet from 1836 until 1857 the march of suburbia had only covered a couple of miles. It was the late Victorian period when the fashion for suburbia took off. Gentlemen working in the city could take well appointed villas away from the smoke, grime and pollution of the city whilst clerks of lower orders would take smaller properties closer to the city – a hierarchy was born.

As the insatiable desire for growth increased, any land close to a railway station became subject to the building prospector. Within a few decades towns and villages grew until they merged into a suburban conglomeration with precious few green breathing spaces. First villages within the ambit of London – Lewisham, Catford and

An official works view of a brand new H class tank locomotive, probably taken at Ashford. The class was designed with suburban traffic in mind, although they found fame on country branch lines towards the end of the steam era. (Courtesy Railway Magazine)

A classic suburban steam train. A Southern Railway M7 locomotive waits at Sevenoaks with three ancient six-wheel coaches. (Photographer unknown, courtesy Railway Magazine)

The sad remains of the former LC&DR built locomotive depot at Faversham. Compare this to the thriving scene on page 40. Following the Kent Coast electrification in 1959 the shed was converted to service diesel locomotives. Following a period when it was used to store rolling stock it was finally abandoned in the 1970s. (Author)

A bustling scene at Faversham where the shed and depot were at the apex of the junction for the lines to Margate (left) and Dover (right). One wonders if the gentlemen in the right foreground are early railway enthusiasts. (W.A. Camwell, R.C. Riley collection)

Blackheath – mushroomed, soon followed by the exploitation of green field sites such as Hither Green. In 1888 Greenwich, Woolwich, Lewisham and Eltham officially lost their Kentish status to the London County Council. In what might be regarded as a questionable swap, the county gained the joys of Penge in return. Then rural villages and towns in north-west Kent, such as Bexley, Sidcup, Orpington, Bromley and Beckenham, started to enlarge before the entire corner of the county was finally absorbed by suburbia, ultimately becoming divorced from Kent both physically and politically into an area of Greater London. Different areas developed in different ways. Bromley became a more 'upmarket' area with a generally lower density of housing where a couple of prominent landowners did their utmost to bring the railways to the town and exploit the consequences. One, Coles Child, was reaping the best of both worlds, being a prominent railway shareholder as well. Bromley's population grew from 4,100 in 1851 before the first railway arrived to 10,700 thirteen years afterwards. By 1881 its population was almost four times larger than it had been in pre-railway days. By contrast areas to the immediate south of the Thames around Sidcup and Bexleyheath developed along more middle or working class lines with tidy, yet less upmarket properties. Sidcup's population exploded nearly six-fold after the arrival of the railway in 1866. It is a curious quirk of history that today in the middle of a bland suburban high street a proud building or ancient church, a reminder of a bygone village past, still stands cheek by jowl with far less worthy later buildings.

The commuter from Kent from the outset was well served by a choice of Central London destinations: Cannon Street, Blackfriars and Holborn Viaduct in the City and Charing Cross and Victoria in the West End. Commuters from few other counties had such a choice of destinations (whatever they thought – or still think – of the service offered!). Hence Kent became prime commuter land in comparison with, for example, Essex, which can only offer two terminals on the eastern periphery of the City of London. With a build up of passenger traffic the railway (not always successfully) strove to increase capacity and any improvement in service was matched by a further rise in passenger numbers as estate companies promoted an easier or quicker journey to work. The original twin track viaduct out of London Bridge was ultimately widened to accommodate 13 lines in places, whilst the main line as far out as Orpington was quadrupled in 1904. Landowners were still up to their old tricks – land for widening near Chislehurst Tunnel was only sold on condition that a new station at Elmstead Woods would be added. The existing tunnel (only included to appease the landowner in the first place) had been built of necessity so close to the surface that it started to collapse when work started to build the second tunnel next to it. On the other hand Dulwich College was wealthy enough not to sell, hence the 'Chatham' main line through Dulwich and Penge remains to this day only double track.

Many building promoters worked with the railway. New Beckenham and Lower

Locomotive No 31405 dashes through Bickley cutting with an August Bank Holiday Monday excursion in 1957. Bickley became one of the leafiest and most upmarket creations in suburbia with large houses set in extensive grounds. (R.C. Riley)

Sydenham stations on the Addiscombe line (today the trains go to Hayes) were built as part of an overall housing deal with the Cator Estate. A new station on the Bexleyheath line called Shooters Hill and Eltham Park was opened in 1908 at the instigation of the Corbett Estate. As the new estates moved ever outwards from London, the old adage that the better job you had, the further out you lived came to fruition as after the First World War enormous London County Council housing estates were built in the inner suburban area at Kidbrooke and Downham near Bromley, the latter served by Bellingham and Grove Park stations. During construction the Downham Estate included a significant internal railway system to move construction materials around.

A classic study of a South Eastern & Chatham Railway express, date and location unknown. (Photographer unknown, courtesy Railway Magazine)

The remorseless stimulation of unbroken building growth continued unabated and was even hastened by the onset of electrification in the 1920s and 1930s, only to be abruptly terminated by the buffer stop of post-war green belt policy.

Away from the metropolis, existing towns within easy travelling distance began to change their nature, becoming 'dormitory towns' such as Sevenoaks, Tonbridge and the Medway towns. As rail travel became faster and housing stock closer to London, more expensive and in shorter supply, so the phenomenon spread further out into the county.

The Only Way To Go

An invitation to Kent. This poster from the 1950s shows that even British Railways was keen to exhort passengers out into the county for some hearty fresh air. (National Railway Museum/ Science and Society Picture Library)

For most of the age of steam the railway had the benefit of a virtually captive audience. There was simply no other practicable means of conveying passengers and freight overland so efficiently and conveniently. Travel by road was cumbersome and for the vast majority of the population was still horse powered until the 1920s. Conveyance of bulk loads by sea was the only other option, where geography permitted.

KENT RAILWAYS

VICTORIAN PERSONALITIES

In the early days of the railways in Kent some of the best known personalities in the country were regular travellers who also took a keen interest in the building and operation of the system. The Duke of Wellington, famous as the victor over Napoleon at Waterloo in 1815, subsequently became Prime Minister and was infamously hostile to the railways on the grounds that it was inappropriate for the lower classes to have the ability to travel. He considered the whole affair could end up in revolution. He did, however, attend the opening of the Liverpool & Manchester Railway in 1830 and in due course his attitude mellowed. In 1839 he took up office as Lord Warden of the Cinque Ports, his official residence becoming Walmer Castle. When the SER was pushing towards Dover he took the opportunity to inspect the tunnel at Shakespeare Cliff, walking the whole length of both bores. Once the railway was open to Dover he became a regular traveller to London. He had his own private carriage provided, once making a formal complaint when his train was an hour late. The day before he died in 1852 he was inspecting construction work at Dover's Admiralty Pier. The news of his death reaching Apsley House in London was by 'private message of the telegraph of the South Eastern Railway'. In due course the SER charged his estate £90 for assisting with the funeral arrangements.

Charles Dickens took a keen interest in the railways, at times speaking at dinners and celebrations held to mark the opening of new lines. Dickens lived at Broadstairs and latterly close to his childhood home at Higham near Rochester. He was a familiar face on the railways and being the 19th-century equivalent of an 'A list celebrity' had its advantages. In 1854 he wrote: 'Leaving Calais on the evening of Sunday, the 10th of December; fact of distinguished author's being abroad was telegraphed to Dover; thereupon authorities of Dover Railway detained train to London for distinguished author's arrival, rather to the exasperation of the British public.' A decade later, in June 1865, a return from a Continental journey had a much darker and more profound experience when he was a passenger on the train that was involved in the most ignominious accident to occur in the history of the railways in Kent. At this time the Continental steamers were still dependent on the tide and the connecting boat trains were accordingly affected. A bridge at Staplehurst across the River Beult was being renewed and the foreman in charge misread the timetable and authorised the removal of the bridge's timber beams at a time when the Continental express was due. His error was compounded when he placed the look-out too close to the bridge. Ten people were killed and 40 seriously injured when the bridge collapsed under the weight of the train. Dickens wrote to an old school friend Thomas Mitten: 'I was in the only carriage that did not go over into the stream. It was caught upon the turn by some of the ruin of the bridge, and hung suspended and balanced in an apparently impossible manner ... Looking down I saw the bridge gone and nothing below me but the line of the rail … The two guards (one with his face cut) were running up and down on the down side of the bridge (which was not torn up) quite wildly … came upon a staggering man covered with blood (I think he must have been flung clean out of the carriage) with such a frightful cut across the skull that I couldn't bear to look at him. I poured some water over his face and gave him some to drink, and gave him some brandy, and laid him down on the grass, and he said "I am gone" and died afterwards. Then I stumbled over a lady lying on her back against a little pollard tree, with the blood streaming over her face (which was lead colour) in a number of distinct little streams from the head. I asked her if she could swallow a little brandy, and she just nodded, and I gave her some and left her for somebody else. The next time I passed her, she was dead. No imagination can conceive the ruin of the carriages, or the extraordinary weights under which people were lying … in writing these scanty words of recollection, I feel the shake and am obliged to stop.'

For most of the steam age the railway mirrored society with a passenger's journey being strictly first, second or third class. However, at the station it was usually different, although in the early days different classes of waiting room were sometimes provided and a first class distinction survived longer at some of the larger termini.

THE STATIONS

What sort of station was provided for the Kentish traveller? The South Eastern Railway had an odd reputation for the quality of its stations. Its hallmark was mean wooden clapboard structures with associated signal boxes and huts built to a similar design. Some of these wooden signal boxes, with their large sash windows and hipped roofs, looked quite stylish. In complete contrast some stations were built in highly attractive classical, Italianate, Gothic or Tudor styles. It is curious that the same line could have a random mix of several different styles. The wooden ones were built in the 1840s and again after 1860. They were distinctive and, if anything, portrayed a running 'house'-style building theme, although calling it an architectural style may be pushing the boundaries. The SER even built a wooden hotel in the style at Port Victoria in the Isle of Grain. Over the years, only a few of them have survived in contrast to many pleasing Gothic, Italianate and Tudor examples, which are still liberally dotted around the system. The Tudor designs featured in the late 1840s and were refined through the 1850s with a mix of Gothic and Italianate.

The SER never really got to grips with a flagship station design. London Bridge, its headquarters, was always being chopped and changed around and when a pleasant permanent façade was finally erected, it gave the impression of being subsumed by the activity around it instead of commanding its position. Badly bombed in the Second World War, it spent the following 30 years as a baleful eyesore until demolished in 1976. At Dover, an impressive terminus was designed but nothing was actually built

A classic example of a South Eastern Railway wooden clapboard station: wooden buildings, wooden canopy, wooden shed, wooden signal box. This is a deserted Hythe station, terminus of the branch line from Sandling with H class 31521 awaiting departure on 28th August 1951, four months before the line closed. (R.C. Riley)

on a grand scale. The SER preferred to channel its efforts into its hotel, the Lord Warden. Over the years, interaction with the LC&DR saw various Dover stations in different locations, although at times passengers were just decanted onto the dockside. It was not until the post Edwardian period, when the warring companies were being jointly managed, that a long overdue prestigious maritime terminus was built although its opening was delayed until after the First World War. It survived as a station until 1994. Today, with its tracks tarmaced over for road vehicles, it has been refurbished for use as a cruise terminal.

The LC&DR went for a more simple brick style of station, usually with the stationmaster's house as part of the whole. The earliest ones were more like a residential Victorian villa built as a wayside station with the usual facilities incorporated into the design, and a canopy or awning to provide shelter on the platform. The stations on the line between Otford and Maidstone were built to a more compact and pleasing plan – they looked like the first stations the Chatham had designed as 'stations' as opposed to railway-side houses. All except Barming were rebuilt soon after, becoming much enlarged with high gables and an integral station house. As a result, their appearance dramatically changed and they too looked more like large detached Victorian houses, especially when viewed from the side facing away from the railway.

The railways were always adept at promoting their services. Bold posters would advertise cheap fares to London or the local market town whilst more artistic examples would tempt would be travellers off to the coast for the day. Once through the station doors, a ticket was bought at a hatch so small that most of the booking clerk was hidden from view, let alone the inner sanctum of his office. With the county fielding two of the earliest railways in the entire country, one of the first lines even pre-dated the concept of the ticket. The London & Greenwich issued metal tokens sold by a 'money taker' that was surrendered at the end of the journey. This was workable for a simple line but not when things got more complicated. The Canterbury & Whitstable was more imaginative. In 1834 the directors announced: 'To meet the wishes of many individuals, the Directors have resolved to issue Family and Personal tickets for the season from Lady Day to 1st November. Each Personal Ticket will cost Two Guineas and Each Family Ticket will cost Five Guineas', thus claiming the first seasons tickets (and perhaps the first family railcard) in the world!

Opened by the London, Chatham & Dover Railway in 1874, Barming station retains the only unrebuilt wayside station building between Otford and Maidstone. (Author)

An example of the London, Chatham & Dover Railway wayside station. This is Shepherdswell where the station house has been built at right angles to the railway. Class O1 locomotive No 31258 brings a Railway Enthusiasts' Club special off the East Kent Railway into the main line station on 23rd May 1959. (R.C. Riley)

R.E.C.
31258
SPL
77
GENTLEMEN
LET THIS
SITE
WELL

TOP END TRAVEL – DAY AND NIGHT

The steam age in Kent saw an astounding variety of passenger trains from the high profile 'Golden Arrow' on the one hand to very much down at heels workmen's trains on the other. The international rail-sea-rail journey from London to Paris was the icing on the cake and over the years the Continental traffic has been handled at a variety of ports. This traffic encompassed all classes and by the 1920s luxury trains were being named in what would now be called a branding exercise. Pullman cars, initially an American concept, had seen limited use in Kent since 1892 either singly or in pairs on the faster passenger trains or very occasionally as all Pullman 'club car' expresses. In the 1920s the Southern Railway introduced an all-Pullman boat train, upgrading it in 1929 to a package including a bespoke first class ship, the *Canterbury*, for the Channel crossing. The 'Golden Arrow' was born. Victoria was now the London terminus chosen for Continental traffic and departure at 11 am would see a Paris arrival at 5.30 pm. This was fine if Paris was a final destination, but of no use for top end luxury connections to the rest of Europe or the Orient as these trains left the other side of Paris in the mornings. The solution to this problem was the inauguration in October 1936 of one of the lesser known but fascinating trains to travel through both Kent and the entire UK – the 'Night Ferry'. Until the opening

A very rare photograph of a 1930s boat train at speed near Sandling; note the single Pullman car. The locomotive is an L class. Although the resulting print has deteriorated over the last 80 years, it is unusual to find such a well composed picture of a train at speed taken at this time. (Original photographer unknown, courtesy Railway Magazine)

The Golden Arrow, 11th October 1951. The official caption to this photograph reads: 'Mr J. Elliot, chairman of British Railways, inspecting the locomotive William Shakespeare before it left Victoria this morning'. One of the new Britannia class standard locomotives, this had spent much of the year on exhibition at the Festival of Britain on the South Bank; the Golden Arrow was considered an appropriate train for the celebrity locomotive to haul. (British Railways, Southern Region)

of the Channel Tunnel at the close of the 20th century this remained the UK's only international passenger train. Utilising the Dover–Dunkirk train ferry, sleeping cars belonging to the Compagnie Internationale des Wagons-Lits operated a through London to Paris service every night, leaving Victoria around 10 pm. Twelve cars were specially built to the UK loading gauge together with three train ferries named after crossing points on the River Thames – the 'Twickenham Ferry', the 'Hampton Ferry' and the 'Shepperton Ferry'. Fares were astronomical for the times (£9 4s return first class) and the shunting of the sleeping cars on and off the ferries plus the necessity to chain them to the shipboard tracks made it an insomniac of a train. Yet it enjoyed a clientele that would match the genuine 'Orient Express' of old. The original Orient Express was one of the grand trains that could now easily be caught onwards from Paris. Uniquely, customs and immigration facilities were provided at Victoria, the

After the Second World War there was an attempt to give the luxury Pullman cars a slightly more contemporary feel. The official caption reads: 'Interior of the modernised Pullman car Malaga which will eventually be placed in the Golden Arrow Service. Extensive use has been made of anodised aluminium for the interior decoration with Australian wax walnut finish. In addition hand-carved aluminium plaques have been fitted in the saloon and coupe compartment. The carriage has been posed at Stewarts Lane depot in 1949. (British Railways, Southern Region, courtesy Railway Magazine)

Once the Pullmans were on the way out, their replacements were considerably less appealing. The Southern Region's publicity office merely titled this picture a 'First class refreshment car'. (British Railways, Southern Region, courtesy Railway Magazine)

train being effectively bonded throughout its journey in the UK. Only one person managed to break the requirement. Winston Churchill saw absolutely no reason why he should travel up to London when the Night Ferry would then return non-stop back through his local main line station at Sevenoaks. He insisted it be stopped for him there and it did, but the entire station had to be closed to everyone else in the process. The Night Ferry provided a Pullman car for the provision of breakfast on the British side whilst in France only the Continental version was available from the sleeping car attendants!

Of course it was not just the elite who travelled by train as part of their international journey. The age of steam was also the age where there was no realistic alternative to rail travel through Kent as part of any journey that involved crossing the Channel. All classes of passenger were catered for and the competition for the traffic was intense. The SER had bought derelict and silted up Folkestone Harbour as an effort to both start a cross Channel service as soon as possible and also to be free of restrictions from the Admiralty and Harbour Board at Dover. Integral to this was the lease or purchase and operation of its own steamers. The LC&DR introduced its own cross Channel service in 1862. Unlike the intense warfare between the two companies that waged on land, a more mature approach was initially attempted on the shipping front. Inevitably, it was doomed to failure. As soon as the Chatham set up in opposition the two protagonists agreed to pool receipts on international traffic under the 'Continental Agreement'. Essentially this involved a 68% / 32% split in favour of the SER on all traffic using the Channel ports south of Margate. Of course, over the years, it became the source of endless bickering and disagreements.

QUEEN VICTORIA, PORT VICTORIA AND QUEENBOROUGH

Queenborough by the Medway estuary on the Isle of Sheppey was outside the agreement and the LC&DR's pier was the point of embarkation for a cross Channel steamer service to Flushing. In response to this, the SER found sudden enthusiasm for a line being locally promoted across the Isle of Grain. In a classic example of how to annoy the neighbours, the SER took over promotion of the line and carried it on to an isolated point on the other side of the Medway opposite Queenborough where a large port was planned. For the want of anything else to call it, the isolated place was named 'Port Victoria'. It had a deepwater frontage and no matter what the state of the tide was, ships of up to 18 ft draught could come alongside. In true South Eastern style a wooden pier with a wooden station, and this time even a wooden hotel (at a cost of £1,900), were quickly thrown up. The SER then spent years baiting the 'Chatham' by attempting to unsuccessfully woo Dutch and Belgian operators

Jutting out into the Medway estuary, the bleak and windswept wooden pier and station at Port Victoria. (Original photographer unknown, courtesy Railway Magazine)

away from Queenborough. A ferry was also provided to Sheerness. Despite being 12 miles closer to London Charing Cross than Sheerness and Queenborough were to London Victoria, commercially Port Victoria was a spectacular flop and only saw any meaningful use when Queenborough Pier was put out of action by fire. The remote location did find favour with one family – the Royal Family. Queen Victoria found it entirely satisfactorily located, being both far away from prying eyes and also the closest deep-sea embarkation point from Windsor Castle. Whether she was unduly influenced by the name bestowed upon the place is unrecorded. Port Victoria became the preferred route for trips involving the Royal Yacht and the Royal Train, including the visits of royalty and dignitaries from abroad. Luck was never on Port Victoria's side. In 1896 major work was undertaken following a marine worm infestation on the pier's piles, only for the whole structure to be further damaged in a severe storm later that year, and then for dredging work to expose more timbers to infestation. Ultimately the SER gave up the unequal battle and leased it to the Royal Corinthian Yacht club. In due course the shipping operators gave up on Queenborough as well, transferring operations to Harwich in Essex, which in due course became one of the major ports in the UK. The 1930s saw the pier cut back and replaced by a spartan landward station, its only passengers being workers on the oil refineries that rapidly developed in this corner of the Isle of Grain. The structure was finally demolished during the Second World War although traces of the piles are still visible today at low tide. Ironically the area adjacent to Port Victoria has now become the deep-water container port of 'Thamesport'. The single track railway branch that was built to Port Victoria is now one of the most intensively used freight lines in the UK with block container trains connecting the north of England to the port. Perhaps Edward Watkin's ghost can be heard chuckling after all.

DIRTY TRICKS AND A SHINGLE WILDERNESS

The South Eastern's most outrageous attempt to avoid paying into the 'Continental Agreement' pool was to rebuild the station at Shorncliffe, then on the outskirts of Folkestone, detrain passengers there and claim that the station was not in Folkestone and therefore outside the agreement. Exactly what the hapless passengers – mere pawns in the argument – thought of this is unrecorded but it did not fool the House of Lords who ordered the SER to pay over £50,000 into the 'pool', following a protracted legal battle. Tellingly today Shorncliffe station is known as Folkestone West. Undeterred, the South Eastern started thinking about building new ports at Littlestone and Dungeness in order to frustrate the agreement even further. The arrival of the railway at the remote south-east tip of the county at Dungeness was probably the ultimate in money wasting excesses. There seems little justification for it other than 'it might have been a good idea'. Today the area has a reputation for stark beauty, albeit overshadowed by two nuclear power stations. In the 1880s there was absolutely nothing apart from a tiny ramshackle fishing community, an Admiralty signalling station and a lighthouse. The Romney Marsh has been dubbed the eighth continent and its seaward tip at Dungeness, comprising nothing but hundreds of acres of shingle, is its backyard. There was no reason to build a railway apart from Watkin's vague ideas about constructing a new port, which itself was a dubious proposition given the constantly shifting shingle. Nonetheless a new line was built from a junction off the Ashford–Hastings line at Appledore. A branch off the branch also served New Romney. Until the 1920s the shingle was excavated in bulk and taken away to be used as railway ballast until the practice was outlawed after a fatal accident at Sevenoaks in 1927 was attributed in part to its lack of suitability for the job. That the railway lasted for as long as half a century is surprising. In 1937 the Southern Railway closed the furthest section to Dungeness and re-sited the New Romney part nearer the sea. This spurred the development of holiday camps at Greatstone and Littlestone, the line surviving until 1967. The only lasting legacy of the railway coming to Dungeness was the bringing of redundant carriages down from Ashford works. Separated from their wheels, the bodies were dotted around the shingle wastelands to become rough new homes for the fishing community. Scores of them are still there today. Again in another irony, the line survives to the closest remaining point to Dungeness to this day, to convey nuclear waste from the power station. Another example of Watkin's excesses serving an unforeseen use in the 21st century.

KENT RAILWAYS

THE CLASS SYSTEM ON WHEELS

Passenger accommodation on boat trains had been dismal; a commentator once described an SER boat train as having the appearance of a moving 'castellated wall', such was the non standard appearance of the rolling stock. It was only in 1852 that second and third class passengers were provided with lights in their carriages. Only in the 1890s were toilets introduced and it was not until the 1920s that improved third class stock was built, featuring gangways and corridors. At Dover a state of the art terminal called Dover Marine had been planned in the pre First World War years but it opened to the public only when Continental traffic resumed after the armistice. For the previous 50 years Dover passengers had transferred from train to ship on the quayside with only rudimentary shelter – or none at all – to protect themselves from whatever gales were whipping in off the English Channel.

As well as the Continental traffic there were some premium expresses that served Folkestone and the coastal Thanet towns. From an early stage they were tied in with commuter traffic. The Kent coast is one of the first places where 'gentlemen who busied themselves in the city' chose to live a long way from the capital. As early as 1896 a 'City Express' linked Holborn Viaduct with the Thanet coast, leaving at 5.10 pm and running non-stop to Westgate-on-Sea at 6.46 pm and Ramsgate at 7.05 pm – 21st-century passengers may care to compare their journey times! Curiously there was no 'up' working until 1898 when a 7.45 am departure from Ramsgate would see arrival in the City at a civilised 9.48 am. For the leisure market other named expresses travelled in the opposite direction such as the 'Thanet Belle' to Margate and the 'Man of Kent' via Folkestone. There was even a short-lived 'Kentish Belle' to Canterbury.

For the extremely well off, first class Pullman travel was the epitome of luxury. The first Pullmans in Kent were introduced in 1892. American built and shipped over as a kit of parts, they ran firstly to Dover and Canterbury via Ashford and also to Hastings. A few years later a Pullman express from Folkestone to London was introduced. The Pullmans were owned and operated by an independent company and set exemplary standards of carriage comfort with service by uniformed attendants. The glossy image of today's restored 'Orient Express' really does reflect the reality of everyday travel for the affluent traveller in the age of steam who could sit in a deep armchair amid the splendour of wood panelling and intricate marquetry, enjoying the best cuisine on rails. Next down the pecking order was the first class passenger who would enjoy comfort and surroundings far removed from the plastic finish and neon glare of the 21st-century carriage interior. For main line commuters the length of their journey is much the same today as it was in the steam age – the fastest journey times from London to the Kent coast remained virtually unchanged after the railway was electrified from the days of the post-war steam express, hauled by Bullied's 4-6-2

One of the famous named trains was the 'Man of Kent'. 'West Country' class 34021 Dartmoor passes London Bridge with the 1.08 pm Charing Cross–Folkestone on 14th May 1959.
(R.C. Riley)

'Battle of Britain' and 'West Country' locomotives.

Away from the luxuries of first class and the prospect of a pleasant seaside home, commuting became less bearable. The reality of a daily suburban commute by steam was characterised by old rolling stock, dirt, soot and grime. The Greenwich line had kick-started the daily commute and the SER was not slow to capitalise upon it. In 1849 a first class annual season from Gravesend to London cost £26 5s. House building within walking distance of a station was encouraged by the offer of initial free season tickets and favourable rates to the builder for the conveyance of his building materials.

In contrast to the impressive yet somewhat impersonal main line expresses or the horrors of a grimy commute there was the country branch line where life went on at a different pace. Although the branch line in the age of steam has a bucolic image, it was just as important to the rural economy as its main line counterpart to the towns and cities. There was also significant travel between intermediate local stations on the main lines.

DAYS OUT

Excursions and special trips by train have been a feature of the railways since a Mr Thomas Cook first booked a private train in Leicestershire. In many ways they offer a glimpse of the social interests of their age. As early as 1844 the SER started running weekend excursions from Bricklayers Arms (a South London terminus built as an unsuccessful alternative to London Bridge) to Dover in an attempt to keep third class passengers off its better long distance services. Only in 1881 did the South Eastern agree to add third class carriages to all its ordinary trains – of course, the very poor and destitute could not afford to travel at all. In the 1850s the SER was desperate to capitalise on excursion traffic. The sport of prize fighting had been made unlawful and driven away from its city roots to areas where the authorities might have more trouble controlling such events. Some fights were held in remote areas in the countryside and the SER was only too happy to run excursions to these ad hoc venues. In 1850 one such excursion was run to a venue in fields near Edenbridge where the train stopped and steps were provided down the embankment for the punters' convenience. A month later the same arrangements were disrupted by the police, but everyone simply jumped back on the train, which then stopped on the way back to London at a suitable venue for the event to be concluded. For nearly 20 years this remained a lucrative trade with venues as far afield as Appledore served by special excursions. The South Eastern compounded its frustration of the authorities by refusing to allow the police access to the railway telegraph and turned a blind eye to the protests of the government until the running of such excursions was made unlawful after 1868. At the other end of the moral plane were the excursions to the Great Exhibition of 1851. The bulk of visitors went by special train and the SER ordered 60 new carriages for the purpose. Cheap seaside excursions were an evergreen source of income. Ramsgate and Margate were targeted remorselessly in competition with the steamers and were so profitable that protests at running such bawdy entertainments on a Sunday were met with deaf ears.

Special workmen's trains are not usually associated with Kent, but bespoke services were provided for miners working in the Kent coalfield. The mines operated three shifts during every 24 hours and some of the oldest and grubbiest rolling stock was provided to take them to and from work at Chislet and Snowdown collieries at all times of night and day to coincide with the changing of the shifts. These trains usually ran from the collieries to Dover, Canterbury or Margate. If the Night Ferry was a train at one end of the scale unique to Kent, then at the opposite end were the infamous hop pickers' specials.

HOPS & ROBBERS, MUCK & MINES

A HOP INTO KENT

Hops and Kent have been inexorably linked for centuries. The oast house with its distinctive cowl built for drying hops after picking is the most iconic piece of architecture in the county. Hop gardens (however large a field of hops is in Kent, it is always referred to as a garden) still feature prominently in the landscape, although not to the extent that they once did. The harvesting of hops at the end of summer is a particularly labour intensive operation and it was only with the coming of the railways that it was possible to transport on mass the numbers of people required for the work. Before the railways those who sought hopping work were constrained by the distance they could walk. Not many were able to make use of a horse and cart. Comparatively few made it to the areas around the River Medway and the Weald that later became synonymous with the invasion of seasonal workers, and this would involve sleeping rough and probably begging on the journey. The source of the workforce was families from the impoverished areas around Rotherhithe, Bermondsey and Deptford, although there were some pickers from a wider area around London's East End. Often it was the women and children who came; men who had work at home usually stayed at their normal jobs. For many it was a time honoured tradition, with the same families returning to the same farm year after year, generation after generation, for a couple of weeks paid work in the countryside. Whilst the locals claimed to be scandalised by the activities of the annual autumnal invasion (petty crime did increase but major incidents were rare) local shopkeepers and traders nonetheless profited handsomely. A local clergyman chose to describe the annual influx thus: 'Nothing more squalid can be imagined – they often appear to be one seething mass of rags and tatters.'

Hop picking has often been romantically portrayed as an excuse for a couple of weeks paid work in the fresh air, but the reality is more brutal. In those early years, many of the more impoverished families had no fixed place to live and would leave their accommodation for good to spend the season in Kent. They would have to find new homes on their return. This goes some way to explaining why hop pickers' specials often left London in the very early hours of the morning – it was one night's less accommodation to worry about. It also meant that the pickers thus carried arrived in Kent early in the morning, giving them all day to find their farms and sort out somewhere to work and stay. The other side of the coin was that large numbers of hoppers, often with young families, would arrive stranded at a remote country station with no means of support and would roam the countryside with children and babies in tow until they could find work. Another practical example of the hoppers' dire circumstances was that usually every year fewer hop specials were run 'down' into Kent than returned. This is explained by the fact that significant numbers of people could not afford the fare into the county, but after their work in the hop gardens they could afford the journey back home. In 1880 nearly 19,000 were carried down, but over 22,600 were carried back.

By the turn of the century, social conditions improved and the practice of running the night trains was phased out. The organisation involved in transporting what were then some 30,000 hoppers was a logistical nightmare made all the worse by variations in the hop picking season from farm to farm and year to year. A system was established whereby farmers would keep a record of their 'own' pickers and fill out a postcard telling them when the season would commence on their farm. However, they sent the postcards to a central office of the National Farmers' Union in Maidstone. The NFU would pool the cards and liaise with the railways to establish how many people would need transport to any given station on any given day. Once the railways had worked out how many trains they could scrape together (scrape being the operative word) the NFU would add details of departure points and times to the card and forward them on to the pickers. This would ensure that the correct number of trains would be laid on and departure organisation from whatever point would be less chaotic. Farmers would then bring carts to meet the hoppers on arrival at their destination. With such a sudden requirement to lay on extra trains, all manner of locomotives and rolling stock had to be gathered together. Folklore has it that it was the hoppers' reputation that caused the most elderly and down at heel rolling stock, both in terms of locomotives and carriages, to be provided for them. There may be some truth in this, but the more likely cause is that every available asset had to be utilised given the number of people requiring transportation. Rolling stock was sometimes borrowed from other companies, hoppers occasionally travelling down to Kent in LMS express corridor carriages. The routes were roundabout as well in order to fit the trains around the existing timetable – many went to the Weald via Croydon, Oxted and the long gone Crowhurst spur. The hoppers themselves put up with living accommodation that would be considered unfit for human habitation today. Huts with straw for bedding were the norm, with water from a standpipe or bowser. Most nights were topped off with an enormous bonfire. Little else was provided for them so they had to bring most of their worldly possessions with them, all of which were transported by rail.

It is claimed the first such trains operated by the SER in the 1850s saw the hoppers conveyed in cattle trucks. In the early days, for a fare of 2/6d most left from Bricklayers Arms, which would be inundated with hoppers by 3 am. When that ceased to be used by passenger trains, the hoppers' specials left mostly from London Bridge and New Cross, but also from other stations such as Woolwich and even as far out as Gravesend. They ran to whatever station was closest to the hop garden

What would have been an everyday sight in the early part of the 20th century – hop gardens stretching across the landscape, in places right up to railway lines and station goods yards. On the K&ESR this scene has been recreated (all be it just over the border into Sussex) at Bodiam. (Author)

A returning hop pickers' special passes through Tonbridge station on 15th September 1934. Note the venerable carriages and two vans provided for the hoppers' paraphernalia. (Original photographer unknown, R.C. Riley collection)

SOUTHERN
1159

Marden, a typically rural station in the middle of the hop picking area, which would be seasonally inundated by the arrival and departure of the hoppers. (H.P. White, courtesy Railway Magazine)

their passengers would be working in. This time of year saw many through trains each day to stations on the Hawkhurst branch, usually the preserve of a two-coach local branch train. Even the remaining part of the Kent & East Sussex Railway after it closed to passengers in 1954 still saw hoppers' specials travel along the line when it was usually only open for goods traffic. Paddock Wood was a key hub and the line from there to Maidstone West and the intermediate stations on the main line to Ashford also saw intensive use. It was not just the families who took the train, there were just as many weekend specials put on for 'friends', mostly the menfolk who had remained at their jobs during the week who would travel down on the Saturday afternoon and return on the Sunday evening. The sheer volume of this traffic can be gauged by the fact that on one Sunday evening in 1951 over 20 friends' specials returned to London Bridge in a three and a half hour period.

When the picking season ended and the farmers had decided that the hoppers' labour would no longer be required, the operation was put into reverse, although it was more difficult to load up all the passengers and their possessions at wayside stations where trains behind them would be held up. Hopping continued during the war years for families and those not called up. The start of the Blitz in 1940 saw a further twist on the specials when at the end of the season children were evacuated directly to the north of England without returning home. Marathon long distance return workings included Marden–Birmingham and Wateringbury–Warrington. From both a mechanical and social point of view, it was astounding that the whole pageantry of the exercise lasted as long as it did. In the late 1950s, mechanical harvesting together with generally improving social standards, paid holidays and a greater availability of road vehicles killed the exercise fairly quickly. The last hoppers' special returned to London in 1960. The harshness of conditions and the financial necessity that forced the hoppers into taking their Kentish break is now largely forgotten in the rose tinted mists of nostalgia, yet it was nonetheless one of the most colourful and fascinating aspects of the steam age in Kent.

The oast house is a familiar sight through the carriage window throughout most of the county, and remains so today. This is the 21st century preserved Spa Valley Railway where in a timeless scene both oast house and steam train are seen in the Wealden scenery near Groombridge. This is the border with Sussex; the oast house is in Kent but the train is beyond the county boundary, marked by the line of trees between the two. (Author)

MOVING THE GOODS – DAYLIGHT ROBBERY

The situation in relation to moving goods and freight was the same as for passengers – there was no other realistic alternative to the railway. The top end of the scale for inanimate objects was mail and gold. The South Eastern achieved notoriety for the conveyance of both, but for different reasons. As the fastest method of moving mail from the coast to London, the railways of Kent became the last stage in the transmission of vital information from the far corners of the Empire. Competing newspaper proprietors sometime hired their own trains, although presumably the first to get their story would be the first to have their locomotive or train leave Dover. The Admiralty conveyed the mails across the Channel with the Post Office responsible for transportation across land. Generally the fastest timed trains up from the coast were those that conveyed the 'mails'.

The traffic of Empire also included the export of valuable cargoes, notably gold and silver. This saw Kent becoming the stage for one of the most famous crimes of the 19th century – the 'First Great Train Robbery'. This was a very cleverly planned and executed plot which had all the ingredients for a feature film and not surprisingly one was made in the following century (1979) based on the events, although unfortunately filmed in Ireland as opposed to the county in which it happened. Edward Agar and William Pierce acted together with two 'insiders'. Pierce had been a railway ticket printer and was well aware of the opportunities that presented themselves given the shipment of bullion between London and Folkestone. He shared his ideas with Agar who was a professional criminal of some notoriety. Pierce suggested he could easily obtain the keys to the safes in which the valuables were carried. Agar, under an assumed name, initially bought £200 worth of gold and had it transported by train from London to Folkestone in order to view the operation. In doing this he established that two keys were needed to open each of two locks on each safe in which the valuables were transhipped; one was in the possession of the guard, the other in the possession of the Folkestone stationmaster. He then involved his further accomplices, a roster clerk named William Tester and a guard named James Burgess. Tester was to ensure that Burgess was allocated to the particular train that normally conveyed the bullion. Tester also allowed Agar the opportunity to make a wax imprint of one of the keys when it was temporarily in his custody after it had been returned from alteration by Chubb, the safe manufacturer. In a further stroke of luck, whilst Agar was on one of his recognisance missions to Folkestone a clerk left the second key unguarded in an office cupboard. Agar simply walked it, made another wax impression and left the key where he found it. The problem was that shipments were only random and despite Agar being smuggled by Burgess into his van each time bullion was conveyed, successive imprints of the safe key wouldn't work. He spent many unsuccessful journeys weighed down with lead shot to exchange for the gold.

It all came together for them on the night of 15th May 1855. Three London firms sent gold worth over £780,000 in today's prices to London Bridge for transhipment. The gold was put in the safes in the guard's van and during the journey the switch was made. At Folkestone the criminals had the satisfaction of seeing safes full of lead being offloaded for Paris. Tester was under no illusions and had demanded payment before the operation was complete. He had been passed a bar of gold during the station stop at Redhill. The conspirators stayed on the train to Dover and then returned to London with carpet bags full of gold. As a further security measure the safes were always weighed at each transhipment point, but even with some inconsistencies with the lead weighing less than the gold the crime was undiscovered until the lead reached Paris where the safes were opened. For years the crime went unsolved with accusing fingers being pointed left, right and centre but never in the correct direction. British police blamed the French, French police the British whilst the SER's own police got nowhere. The plot only unravelled when Agar was apprehended for an offence of passing a forged cheque and was sentenced to penal servitude for life. Pierce then stopped financially supporting Agar's common law wife despite being given cash for the purpose. Agar then 'blew the whistle' on his accomplice, having nothing to lose himself. When the matter came to sentencing after trail at the Old Bailey, Tester and Burgess came off much worse as they were deemed to be in breach of trust. They received transportation for 14 years whilst Pierce received a surprisingly lenient two-year sentence.

INDUSTRY AND AGRICULTURE

Today most freight trains operate on a bulk or block conveyance principle, carrying one load a long distance. In the age of steam it was very different. Every station would have at least one siding where good wagons either owned by, or provided by, the railway for individual traders saw products delivered or dispatched. The larger the station, the greater the number of sidings. Some would have a goods shed for the transhipment of products under cover. Special platforms or 'docks' were installed to move animals. Some larger companies would have their own private sidings whilst all the individual wagons would be collected up and taken to larger marshalling yards for distribution to their onward destination, with trains often being re-made up many times over depending on the length of the journey. A local agricultural economy depended upon this method of both importing any raw material needed for production and in turn exporting the finished product. Just about everything went by rail.

The railway was vital for servicing industry. Whilst Kent is generally thought of as a rural county there was, and still is, significant industry in the north-western corner by the Thames and down the Medway Valley towards Maidstone. Here the paper

Moving the goods. Whitstable Harbour in British Railways' days, showing a well loaded train headed one by of the locomotives with a specially cut down cab permitting it to work through Tyler Hill Tunnel on the former Canterbury & Whitstable Railway. Whatever the load, it must be susceptible to water damage as unusually tarpaulins have been provided to cover the wagons. (Rev A.W.V. Mace, R.C. Riley collection)

and cement industries (the latter assisted by local chalk extraction) had established themselves close to navigable rivers. As well as exporting finished products these plants received some raw material in and especially coal to fuel machinery. It was to these areas that the only 'block' trains ran with any regularity, although the industries still made much use of water transport. There were all manner of manufacturing and light industries, many of which utilised private sidings or small internal railway systems. In the 1850s the building of railways themselves even encouraged the growth of the brick industry; in the 1880s one Kentish firm produced 25% of London's standard brick requirements. Much of the industry was situated next to the Thames and its estuary so bricks bound for London went by water, but those inland went by rail. Conversely the coming of the railways could also have an adverse effect upon local crafts and industries as it became cheaper and more convenient to 'import' mass produced products manufactured elsewhere. Whilst the need for bespoke cottage industries was reduced, cheaper goods of all kinds could be brought into the county.

This gave rise to greater 'standardisation' in a whole variety of areas, everything from shopkeeping to building styles. Shops relied more upon factory made and processed items. The ability to depend upon a fixed flow of manufactured items allowed the growth of the multiple 'chain' stores at the expense of the privately owned shop. In house building, for example, Welsh slate began to replace traditional Kentish peg tiles.

Throughout the county there was a whole variety of different types of goods traffic. There was much seasonal fruit to be conveyed from the Kentish orchards. The ability to move dairy products such as milk, butter and cheese quickly prompted a significant increase in the number of cattle being farmed in what had been more remote areas of Kent, especially the Weald. There was a seasonal trade in hops, and fish was carried up from the coast. There was even a trade in manure reclaimed from the streets of London in the days of horse drawn traffic, which was taken

Southern Railway E5X class locomotive 2401 hauls a varied selection of goods wagons towards Canterbury. (Original photographer unknown, courtesy Railway Magazine)

to a purpose-built depot near Fawkham in order to assist the agricultural process afresh! The ability to import not only manure, but also chemical fertilisers, by rail had a further stimulating effect upon agriculture. Before the coming of the railway Kentish farmers had to rely upon locally available supplies, unless they were close to London or a navigable waterway. A further stimulation to agriculture caused by the railway was the growth of suburbia itself. There were now hundreds of thousands of 'consumers' in the north-west corner of the county who formed a ready market for the products grown or produced in the rest of Kent, which was only a short distance away by railway. The livestock market at Ashford was a key animal trading centre with large volumes of cattle and sheep from the nearby Romney Marsh being conveyed by rail. The fertile fields of the marsh allow sheep to graze naturally much more intensively per acre than other parts of the country, a fact reflected in the numbers of animals transported.

BLACK GOLD

No story of the railways of Kent and their industrial connections can be complete without reference to the Kent coalfield. That the county had a substantial coalfield is now a surprise to many people – memories can be short as the last pit closed as late as 1987. In 1880 the first trial borings for one of the many attempts at starting work on a tunnel beneath the English Channel was a failure for its intended purpose but did positively confirm the existence of coal beneath the eastern tip of the county. The early years of the 20th century saw a large number of small pits sunk in a triangle bounded by Ramsgate, Canterbury and Dover. The geology was difficult and many floundered having made no profit, and in some cases having extracted no coal whatsoever.

Ultimately there were four big pits in Kent – Snowdown, Chislet, Betteshanger and Tilmanstone. The first two were already close to main lines, while Betteshanger, near Deal, had a two mile branch line built to it. The main line railway shifted huge amounts of coal out of the area. Tilmanstone was linked (together with several other mines that fell by the wayside) to Shepherdswell by the East Kent Light Railway. This was another of Colonel Stephens' concerns (see Chapter 1), originally promoted in 1910 by the Kent Coal Concessions Company, an amalgamation of 40 different mining interests in the area. At this time pits were being projected throughout the area and from 1911 until 1920 an intricate network of branches linked the various collieries either built, being built or merely planned. The East Kent led a precarious life. Sometimes a short branch was confidently built to a place where a new mine was being sunk, only for no coal to ever be brought to the surface. Other collieries closed very quickly. The First World War saw the building of a brand new port at Richborough, which the East Kent was well placed to serve. Although traffic slumped

One of the East Kent Light Railway's many abortive schemes was to open the branch to Richborough to passenger traffic. Although stations were built, a passenger service was never introduced. At Richborough Port the only passenger facility provided appears to be a bench. It is unsurprising the East Kent never attracted many customers! Perhaps the hoarding facing the road extols the virtues of the new railway. (C.F. Klavone, courtesy Railway Magazine)

again at the end of the war, work progressed on further extensions towards Deal and Canterbury, which ceased on the untimely death of the Colonel in 1931. Just like the Kent & East Sussex Railway, the line was operated by a ramshackle collection of locomotives. Although the emphasis was on shifting large tonnages of coal, passenger services were provided, but they were sparse and were cut back during the economic difficulties of the 1920s. The remaining passenger trains were withdrawn by British Railways in October 1948, only 10 months after nationalisation. By 1951 only the section from Tilmanstone to Shepherdswell survived, lasting until the miners' strike of 1984/5, no coal being mined thereafter. Snowdown closed soon after and had been the last place in Kent where steam locomotives were in use on a daily basis serving industry. Betteshanger was the last Kent colliery to close. Much of the coal went to serve industry in north-west Kent and around the Medway. Most of Chislet's coal was used by the railways themselves and the demise of steam nationally in 1968 is often quoted as the reason for the colliery's closure the following year. It is estimated that 1,000 million tons of coal are still beneath the East Kent downs.

5

Making it Work

Working for the railway in the age of steam was fundamentally different from working on the modern railway of today. As a sole carrier for people and goods over any distance its enormous size and labour intensity meant that a far greater percentage of the population was employed on the railways in comparison with today. In 1914 it was estimated that one in seven of the population of East Kent was reliant on the railway in some shape or form for their employment. It followed that the railway exerted a far greater influence on the lives of the population and a job on the railway was generally viewed by society as having a greater strategic importance. Those who worked on the railway were viewed as vital for the economic good of the county. For employees it was a solid, reliable job – often for life and often covering a span of several generations of the same family.

The earliest lines struggled as men were thrust into key roles in a brand new industry. In the very beginning the London & Greenwich Railway employed a few drivers who had brief experience on the Liverpool & Manchester Railway, which had predated it by about six years. For everyone else it was a steep learning curve. Roles were broadly similar to later years but with some intriguing differences. Guards were exactly that, the term referring to guarding the train or its contents (either passengers or goods) from danger. Their earliest role was to sit in an elevated position at the ends of carriages (there would be several guards) in order to survey the safety of the train. In due course they were also required to double check the driver's compliance with signals. A little known fact is that even up to the 1950s new electric trains were provided with a periscope mounted in the roof above the guard's compartment for this very purpose!

Climbing the tree

Whilst today train operating companies recruit drivers externally with no railway

Contrasts at Dover with the up 'Golden Arrow' hauled by 'Battle of Britain' class 34085 501 Squadron passing D1 class 31505 shunting in the locomotive shed sidings. As far as locomotive crews were concerned the 'top link' passes the 'bottom link'! (R.C. Riley)

experience, in the days of steam it could take a lifetime to reach the upper echelons of the 'top link' driver. There was a rigid grade structure. A boy leaving school would start out as a cleaner, his life being a pre-dawn to post-dusk slog of oily rags, fetching and carrying and loading coal. After several years he might be able to occasionally fire a locomotive out on the line with further years of progression to become a fully passed out fireman, but only on shunting or local freight turns. In due course he would pass up the ranks through local passenger to expresses. Although firemen would take an occasional turn at driving it could take a man half a lifetime to progress to becoming a driver. Then it would be back down to the local goods train and working back up the 'tree', but this time in the driver's seat. Most men only reached the 'top link' of express passenger driving in their 50s. Once the railways in Kent had become established, this pattern of progression repeated itself for a century across the county, from Bricklayers Arms and Stewarts Lane in the west to Ramsgate and Dover in the east. However, some of the top drivers were the stars of their day and there was a lot of truth in the old story that every schoolboy wanted to be an engine driver. There was just little perception about what that entailed.

Basic working conditions, although all is not as it first appears as apparently this railwayman is off to tend his allotment, which according to the official caption he had been doing for the preceding 20 years! The chance to tend vegetables on railway land was one rare perk of working on the railway. (British Railways Southern Region, courtesy Railway Magazine)

A similar rigid system applied in all the other areas. You worked your way up from the bottom. If you wanted to be a signalman you usually started as a box boy running errands and filling in the register of passing trains and signalling movements. Large boxes such as at Tonbridge, Chatham and Ashford would have several boys so employed, although smaller rural boxes would have none. Crossing keepers were entrusted with control of signals protecting their level crossing gates. These were frequently live-in jobs with a house or cottage provided on site, sometimes in remote areas and sometimes where the only water supply was brought in by train. Incredibly, right up until the 1970s the crossing cottage at Warehorne on the Romney Marsh relied on its drinking water being brought in cans filled at Ashford each day and dropped off by a train making a special stop. An outbreak of typhoid was once attributed to a well being used to supply a remote crossing cottage near Rainham.

Working for the railway was considered a good career path. There were hundreds if not thousands of 'railway families' spanning several generations. If a father had a good record as an employee it was almost expected that the company would take on his son if he wanted to follow in his footsteps. A typical example was George Hollands, who led a life on the railways around Kent. His father was signalman at

Tunbridge Wells West with its locomotive shed to the left and goods shed to the right. The former was the scene of many of George Hollands' recollections of working on the railway in the age of steam. On 16th March 1957 L class 31771 departs with a Tonbridge–Brighton train. (R.C. Riley)

Shorncliffe, probably a 1920s' view. A porter seems nonplussed by the passage of an up boat train. The station, venue of the largest dispute over the 'Continental Agreement' the century before, is now known as Folkestone West. (Original photographer unknown, R.C. Riley collection)

Wadhurst and before the Second World War he left school aged 13 and took a first job at Tunbridge Wells Central Goods depot. He progressed to Tonbridge East signal box before taking charge of his own boxes around South London during the height of the Blitz. After the war he returned to Tunbridge Wells, moving to the locomotive department at Tunbridge Wells West depot. He was passed out to drive in 1953 and remained a driver in Kent well beyond the end of steam, finally retiring in 1990. George recalls: 'The road to becoming an engine driver was an often rough one, and paved with pitfalls. A very much sought after job though, with its great prestige and regular monies. But also very crude in its treatment of employees, and so fraught with danger, that the finish of every day's work was such that one mentally and physically breathed a sigh of relief when the handbrake was put on for the last time. The sheer exhilaration and consequent surges of adrenaline that a well driven and fired loco produced had to be experienced to be believed. In all, steam produced a somewhat special type of workforce, and the first few weeks or months of knocking around the shed cleaning engines, and also all the other jobs one was told to do by the shedman soon weeded out those who were unable to stand the strain for the unearthly hours and work. You either loved or hated it. One had to be pretty fit, with a bit of an adventurous spirit, and that weird sense of humour that we had in those far off days, and still have too. The latter was a must, or you didn't survive.'

Signalmen had to be prepared to move around as well since promotion depended upon a steady stream of vacancies becoming available at larger signal boxes. A senior signalman could end his career in charge of the very same large box in which he had started as a box boy. It was a similar pattern at stations, with progression from porter through various grades of booking clerk to stationmaster. Here the career structure always reflected a combination of grade and the size and importance of the station. In the mid 1840s the general weekly pay for a porter was around 18s. At the same time the stationmaster at Pluckley earned 25s, which was less than a booking clerk at Tonbridge who was on 27s, whilst the stationmaster at Marden was on 35s. The Tonbridge stationmaster enjoyed an annual salary of £100.

The stationmaster was an important man in the local community, being the main interface between the 'well to do' and the railway. Whilst some lower grades not seeking promotion remained at the same station for years, most stationmasters, by the nature of their upwardly mobile career intentions, were more transitory. This sometimes led to allegations that they tended to rule their junior grades more harshly as they had less tie to a particular set of employees and saw their future in ingratiating the railway's customers sometimes at the expense of the railway's servants. Such ingratiation could reap rewards – when Ashford's stationmaster retired in 1860 the local passengers clubbed together and presented him with 100 sovereigns (a colossal sum at the time), a silver tray and milk jug! Stationmasters had to live close to their station and the railway usually provided accommodation for them. The quality of housing could vary vastly, from handsome, purpose built villas to unsuitable conversion of existing buildings. In 1909 it was claimed the Sidcup stationmaster was living in a 50 year old converted contractor's hut. Close to the centre of some railway operations, such as major stations or locomotive sheds, housing would sometimes be built for the workforce, with designs and spaciousness rigidly corresponding to the grades and status of employees.

ASHFORD – KENT'S RAILWAY TOWN

In Kent this housing was provided on the largest scale at Ashford, home of the biggest railway works in the county. Whilst Ashford does not owe its existence to the railway, for 150 years it owed its prosperity, growth and most of its employment to it. Until 1846 the locomotive works had been at New Cross, but it had become hopelessly cramped and unable to cope with the requirements of the phenomenal growth that was occurring on the railways in Kent, plus it was also shared with two other companies. The South Eastern Railway looked at building a new 'locomotive establishment' at Tonbridge, Maidstone or Ashford. Maidstone was rejected as being not on the main line and Ashford found favour over Tonbridge as there was more available land — 185 acres were bought in 1846 for £21,000. On the site of 'fields seldom trodden except by the foot of the herdsman' a whole new town was built from scratch to house the enormous workforce required to service the works. Of course the quality and size of each dwelling reflected the respective role of the employees. The most basic accommodation was claimed to be the only 'back to back' houses built in Kent. The workmen's academic needs were catered for by a Mechanics' Institute, which comprised a library and reading room where classes were provided in 'machine drawing, railway carriage building, French, arithmetic and geometry'. There was a public house, which was named the Alfred Arms and a school for 550 pupils was opened in 1852. Everything was planned around a village green. To service the smaller cottages a bath building was put up, on top of which was a 36,000 gallon water tank which also served the works. The SER called the community 'Alfred Town' but the name did not stick; the area became generally known as 'Newtown'. A church was paid for by voluntary subscriptions from the SER's shareholders. By 1912 there were 272 homes.

As well as being home to the works, Ashford was (and still is) a major junction with lines in five directions radiating from the station. Locomotive 1036 hauls two vans away in a westerly direction on 16th July 1934. (A.C. Roberts, R.C. Riley collection)

A reminder of the age of steam – although all is not as it seems. To commemorate the 150th anniversary of the railway reaching Ashford and the significance of the steam locomotive in the development of the town this pair of driving wheels was mounted on the 'green' at Newtown. Despite appearances they are from a scrapped diesel shunting locomotive! (Author)

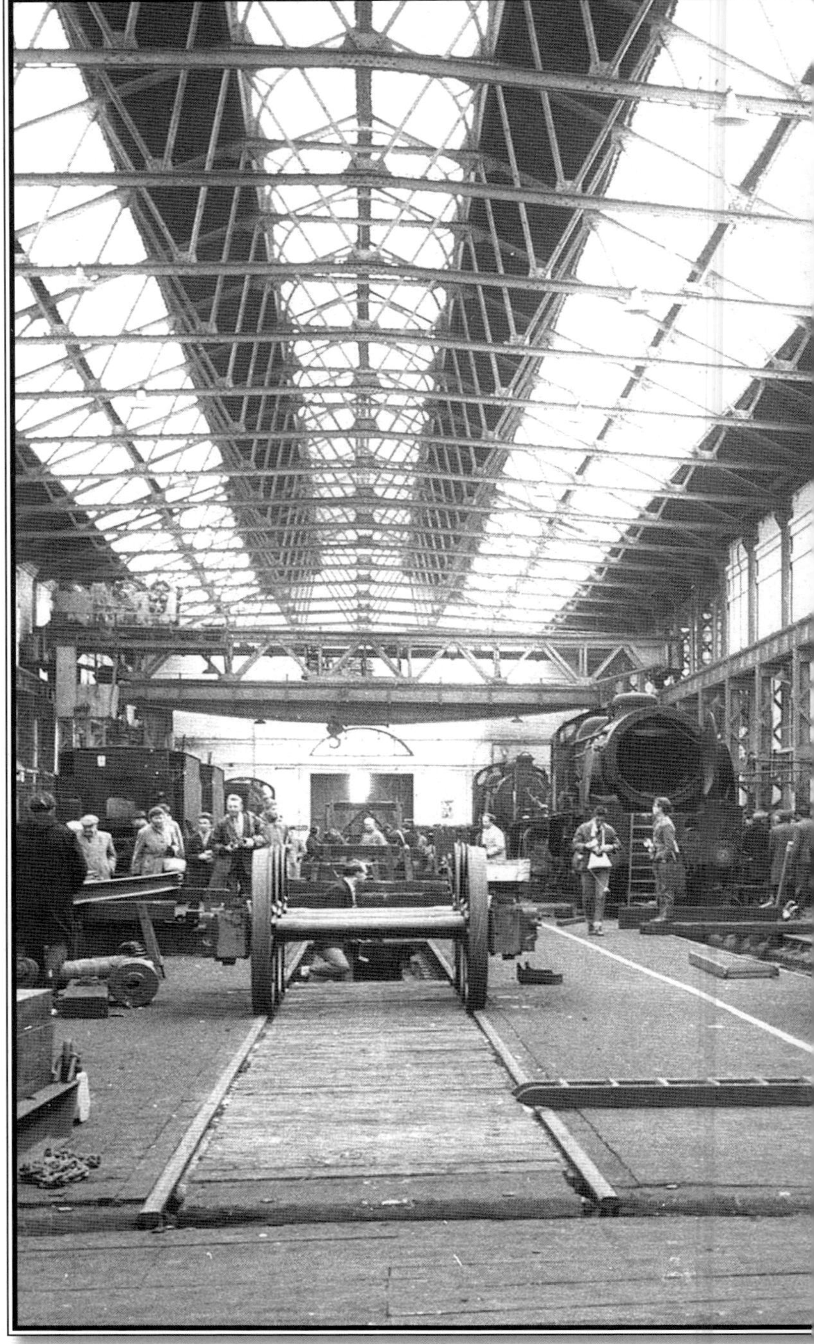

The locomotive works at Ashford on 24th February 1962 with Class N1 locomotives Nos 31862 and 31895.
(L. Sadler, courtesy Railway Magazine)

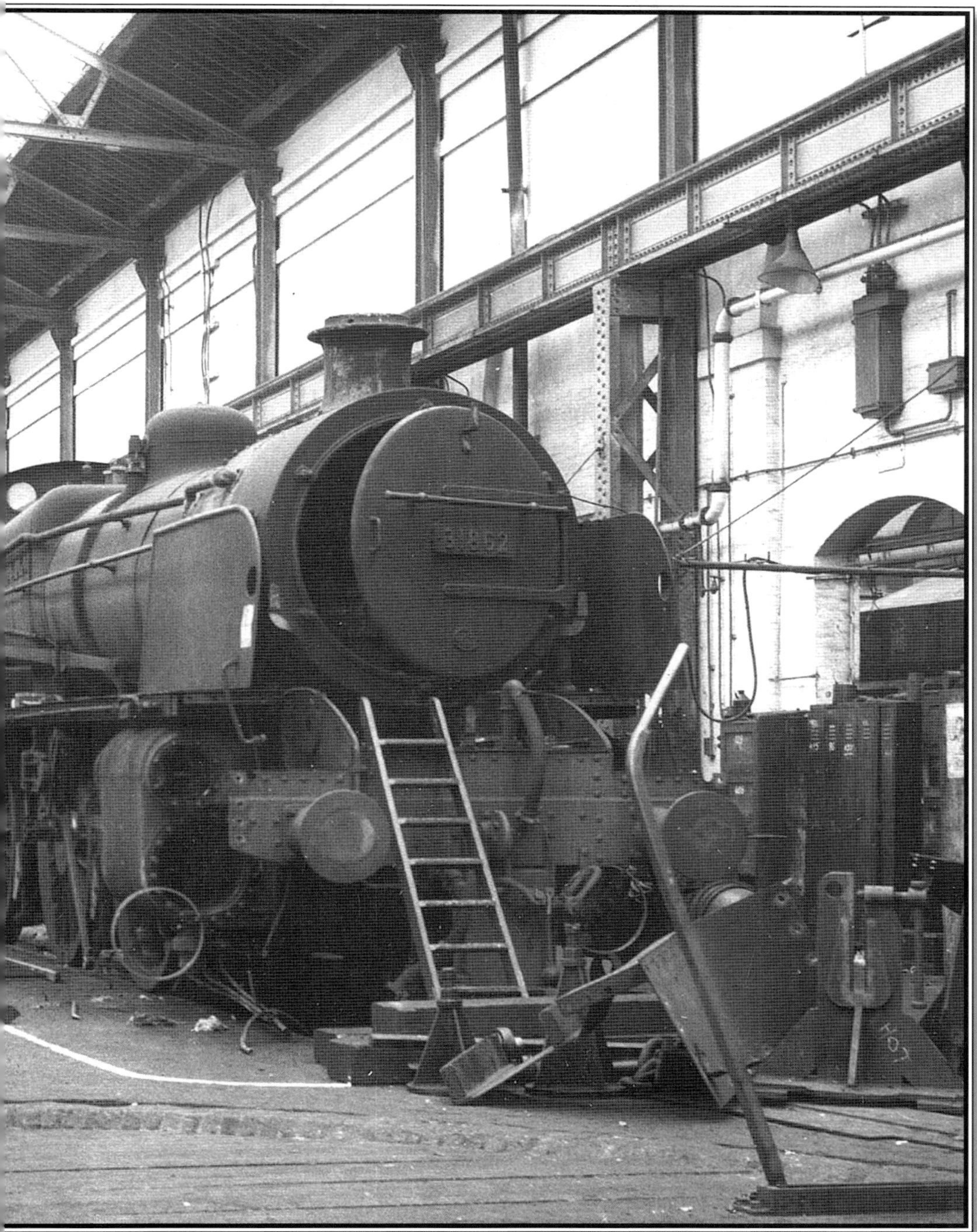

The 1861 *Official Guide to the South Eastern Railway* gives a contemporary indication of immensity of the works: 'These works consist of the large engine shed, 280 feet long by 64 feet wide ... the engine repairing shops and a large crane capable of lifting 20 tons ... machine shop and turnery ... carriage and truck house capable of holding 50 carriages and 80 trucks ... store room ... a perfect model of neatness ... machines – unwieldy and huge in bulk to the most diminutive screw, the whole arranged with greatest precision and elegance.' Over the years more than 1,000 locomotives were built new or extensively rebuilt at Ashford. The works was also responsible for heavy repairs and maintenance. It was also where carriage and wagon building, maintenance and repair was undertaken together with a whole host of other major engineering tasks. It is claimed that 21 descendants of the first coppersmith to be employed at the works were subsequently employed there.

FACT AND FICTION

In the context of employment history the railway companies generally had different reputations. On the whole the South Eastern had a more benevolent attitude than the London, Chatham & Dover although breaches of the rule book were harshly dealt with. The SER was one of the earliest companies to introduce a benevolent fund. The majority of jobs were behind the scenes. Whilst passengers were aware of shadowy figures pulling levers in signal boxes and grime stained men on the footplate they were unaware of the vast legions of workers in

The original Railway Children station as the Railway Children would have known it. Chelsfield station, is seen soon after opening in 1868. Beyond the station can be seen the newly-hewn chalk cuttings. It is not inconceivable that the porter with his platform trolley is the very gentleman that Edith Nesbit wrote about in her novel. (Original photographer unknown, author's collection.)

unseen roles, doing anything from engineering, rolling stock and track repair and maintenance to support office jobs. Yet some of the figures they came to meet and know – those who became the face of the industry to them – were a valued part of their community and their daily lives, for example the lucky stationmaster at Ashford! At the top end of the wage bill came the superintendents or managers, effectively the chief executives. A salary of £2,000 in 1849 was a phenomenal reward, and in the early days senior figures were often paid large sums on a consultancy basis

E class 1176 passes Harbledown near Canterbury in 1946, heading for Faversham with a local train, on the former LC&DR main line from Dover. (Original photographer unknown, Rodney Lissenden collection)

when they were much involved in projects of their own. Frequently the company directors had little knowledge of the workings of the railway; many were industrialists in their own right. However, in the 1850s the SER's James McGregor appointed himself general manager and Sir Edward Watkin frequently involved himself with the everyday direction of the railway, often to the horror of those around him.

Much work on the railway was hard, grim, manual and back breaking. As George Hollands remembers: 'A steam engine was, and still is, a beautiful but unpredictable creature of many moods, never alike two days running, and very dangerous in its extremes. Tunbridge Wells West shed 50-odd years ago was a very different place from what it is now. In the "dead hours" it was a decidedly black and grimy place, with an air of foreboding, as if to say "Wait till I get my hands on you lot". Monday

mornings were sometimes terrors to footplate crews, with limited time for getting an engine ready. This was because all but a few engines had had their fires lobbed out late on Saturday, to be lit up again on the Sunday late turn by a solitary shed fireman. This involved carrying great shovelfulls of red-hot fire across the pits and around the engines, and lifted from ground level up onto the cab floor and then carefully placed under the firebox door. Easier said than done, and often one got scorched if the shovel slipped, sometimes a bit more. Every morn it was like a scene from the middle ages. Flickering torches, with ghostly figures here, there and everywhere climbing onto, under and over the locos.'

Perhaps one of the most famous interactions between railway workers and Victorian society, and a much rosier one, was Edith Nesbit's story, *The Railway Children*. Whilst mostly fictional, the evergreen tale where the children befriended the station porter and enlisted the help of the railway director was actually set at a Kentish station that still survives on the national network today. Many of the incidents in the story were based on factual occurrences. The author lived in a variety of locations around south-east London. Whilst the book was published in 1906 it has been established that it was based on her own childhood recollections of living at Halstead Hall in Kent from 1871–1874. Some commentators have taken this to mean that the station she wrote about was Halstead (now known as Knockholt). This was the point closest to the hall where the children ran down to the line. However, the station there was only built in 1876, which was two years after the Nesbits had left. At the time they lived there the children, drawn by the new technology of the railway and eager to find the nearest station to their house, had discovered the station at Chelsfield, which had opened with the railway three years before they had arrived in the area. Julia Briggs, writing *A Woman of Passion*, a biography of the author, revealed: 'If they ran down the field at the back of the house, they found themselves by the track, which cuts deeply through high banks of chalk, finally disappearing into tunnels in both directions. Walking along the sleepers, as the Railway Children were to do, the Nesbits could follow the line until it finally reached Chelsfield Station, although it was quite tidy walk for them.'

The station still survives and thrives, its claim to fame forgotten. Suburban housing has robbed it of its idyllic country existence. When Edith Nesbit was there, it was surrounded by fields, with strawberries being its greatest export to the capital — milepost 15¼ sits on the platform. The landslide at the conclusion of the story was caused by slippages in the deep, newly-hewn chalk cuttings either side of the station. These are recorded as being of concern to the SER directors of the time; claims about their safety saw Ashcroft, the SER engineer, sue *The Railway Times* and win an apology. Unfortunately none of the structures known to the Railway Children have survived. The classic SER wooden signal box burnt down in 1971, and the timbered main station building suffered significant fire damage two years later and was subsequently rebuilt in steel and glass in 1976. The last building of the Nesbits' time to survive was a large timbered canopy and waiting room situated on the down platform, which BR demolished in 1986, replacing it with the obligatory bus shelter. The coal yard from which the children stole coal was closed to rail traffic in 1964. Station Cottages, home to porter Perks, still exists whilst the tunnel through which the 'paper chase' took place is the curved Chelsfield Tunnel to the south of the station.

6

The Passing of an Age

The image of the steam railway is a wonderfully evocative picture of yesteryear, invoking nostalgia that is fondly embraced by those with memories of the time. For a younger generation it gives the impression of a friendly railway, whilst there is also an admiration of the engineering marvels of the age of steam. Despite all its allure, the reality is the job can be done with greater efficiency and cleanliness by the application of electricity and diesel power. Working conditions in the age of steam would not be tolerated by most people today. A final recollection from George Hollands: 'The job was dirty, draughty and non-hygienic in every extreme. Lobbies were sometimes just short of filthy with only the bare necessities for making tea and chomping on a bit of bread and cheese. Bricklayers Arms was a real "beaut" in those days and my driver and I were treated to the sight of one of the firemen "fishing" for a particularly obnoxious rat under the lockers that lined the paint battered walls. He was doing this with a length of fishing line, a hook and a piece of bread. We watched in fascination as the rat, a big scarred old devil, was hauled squealing and squeaking to his doom under an unforgiving and merciless hobnailed boot. The subsequent squelch caused my mate and me hurriedly to put our sandwiches away until further notice.'

As alternative methods of propulsion developed in the 20th century, railway operators were keen to take advantage of their benefits. An electric or diesel locomotive does not require someone to light it up hours before it is ready to be used. Neither does someone have to spend an hour or so disposing of it, i.e. putting to it to bed, after it has been used – both essentially outdoor work, usually in the early hours of the morning and in all weathers. How many drivers would prefer standing in an open cab with no warmth (other than periodic roasting of the shins when the fire box door is open) to a seat behind a driver's desk in an enclosed, heated cab, sometimes with a cooking ring thrown in! Despite romantic notions, it is doubtful if

A 1946 view of Southern Railway 'West Country' No 21C130 passing Tonbridge with a down express from London Bridge to Dover. A Continental numbering system was used by the Southern Railway when these locomotives were new; in due course it became more conventionally numbered as 34030 and was given the name Watersmeet. (Original photographer unknown, Rodney Lissenden collection)

more than a small number of rank and file railwaymen would have preferred to be on a steam locomotive rather than a diesel at 6 am on a December morning. Perhaps the best example is to consider a domestic comparison. A roaring open fire in the hearth is a wonderful indulgence on a winter's evening. But how many people today would rely on this form of energy for all of their household requirements all day and every day of the year? Like an open fire, the steam locomotive is best viewed through the proverbial rose-tinted glasses – a fundamentally vital building block in the development of transport and now nostalgically revered but obsolete given the march of technology.

The steam locomotive was first ousted from the suburban services running into London. Steam was at its most inefficient on short haul trips that called at many stopping places. The large numbers of locomotives required to operate these trains contributed to the grime and dirt suffered by passengers and to the overall problem of pollution in the London area, which was spiralling out of control in the early and mid 20th century. Electricity was not only cleaner and more efficient but faster. Its greater power of acceleration away from repeated stopping places meant that end to end journey times could be reduced as well. By 1925 the Southern Railway had embarked on an electrification programme that saw steam replaced on inner suburban lines to Hayes, Orpington, Bromley and three routes to Dartford. The writing was on the wall although it would take a further 40 years before steam was finally banished from the county. In many ways it was a period of contrast. Electrical technology gathered pace faster than the progress made to harness diesel power for railway use. Therefore the 1940s still saw three brand new iconic classes of steam locomotive – Bullied's 'Battle of Britain', 'West Country' and 'Merchant Navy' – classes built for express work. These big locomotives were capable of great speed. With the main line expresses capturing the public eye, it was here that the romantic appeal of steam in Kent was at its highest profile at a time when it had already been replaced in other areas.

War weary

By 1939 the third rail had reached both the county town at Maidstone and the Medway towns of Rochester, Chatham and Gillingham. The Southern Railway's aim was an all-electric railway wherever possible. Operational convenience would often see electrification plans drawn up for the smallest branch line. There would be isolated areas where alternative forms of traction would have to suffice – the Southern produced three prototype main line diesels in the 1940s – but electrification wherever practical was the dream. It was a dream, like many others, that was to be shattered by the Second World War. When war was declared the railways immediately came under the control of the Minister for War Transport. The railways of the UK took an unprecedented hammering during the war years, yet nowhere was it more acute than in front line Kent. Troops, munitions and stores had to be carried to and from the Channel ports. Once the German invasion had reached the coast of France and Belgium it became impossible for coastal shipping to ply its trade; the displaced cargoes had to be transported by rail instead, putting an even greater burden on the railways of Kent. There was even a one-way traffic in prisoners of war. Civilians and evacuees had to be conveyed around the county too. All this when the railway was under attack by air and even long range guns from an enemy only miles away across the English Channel.

That the railways rose to such a challenge at a time when all the lines to the coast were powered by steam is phenomenal. The biggest challenge came between 27th May and 4th June 1940, the return of troops of the British Expeditionary Force from Dunkirk. Had the railway not been able to efficiently disperse men quickly out of the Channel ports (and Dover in particular) the resulting log jam would have affected the efficiency of the entire operation. As many as 338,000 men were moved in 586 special trains. The feat was all the more remarkable in that the Southern Railway only received notification of the codeword 'Dynamo' at 5 pm on the evening before the

Today the
infrastructure of the
steam age sees trains
unimaginable to its
Victorian builders. The
nine arch Eynsford
Viaduct was built
in 1862. In 2010
a train conveying
nuclear waste from
the power station
at Dungeness to
Sellafield in Cumbria
for reprocessing
crosses the distinctive
structure. (Author)

operation commenced. Providing food and drink for the troops was accomplished by stopping at wayside stations with passing loops such as Faversham, Headcorn and Paddock Wood where volunteers would have about 15 minutes to serve an entire train through the carriage windows before it would set off again with the next one immediately behind. During the stops, postcards would be handed out to be filled and collected at the next stopping point for onward transmission to families and friends. This would be the first opportunity to inform loved ones that their menfolk had been safely evacuated off the Dunkirk beaches. There was such a shortage of cups that tea was provided in tin cans, which had to be thrown out of the carriage windows when the train set off, there being no time to collect the 'empties' in a more orderly fashion. A lesser known achievement is that there was a simultaneous evacuation of children out of Kent, which had started only a few days earlier when it was realised that their safety was no longer guaranteed given the proximity of the enemy in France.

During the Blitz the railways in the north-western corner of the county suffered heavily, but the entire county was in 'bomb alley', with huge tonnages of explosive being dropped prematurely either by accident or design en route to their intended destination. Some south-east Londoners took nightly refuge in the huge network of caves at Chislehurst, the adjacent station seeing hundreds of people commuting nightly. On the night of 29th/30th December 1940 the old SER station building at London Bridge was burnt out in a fire raid. The blackout was rigidly enforced; station lighting was much reduced and at one stage passengers endured their entire journey in darkness until regulations forbidding any kind of lighting in carriages was relaxed. The bombing of railway hubs in Kent was also a key aim of the Luftwaffe. Even passing passenger trains were strafed by German fighters. On one occasion six fighter aircraft concentrated their attack on the footplate of a moving train near Deal. Occasionally the terrified train crew could take refuge in the nearest tunnel, the selection of tunnels in the Dover area being particularly fortuitous. On 26th November 1942 near Lydd on the New Romney branch a low flying German fighter fired on a locomotive. Its boiler was pierced and it is claimed that the emptying jet of steam brought down the low flying attacker, with the pilot being flung out and drowned in a ditch. The aircraft was destroyed yet the locomotive was repaired. The railway also fought back with anti-aircraft guns mounted on armoured trains deployed at Tonbridge and Canterbury.

When peace returned the railway was in a ghastly state – damaged, exhausted, under invested and worn into the ground. Under the post-war Labour government nationalisation followed, it being claimed that any attempt to recover would be too much for a private company. The Southern Railway became part of British Railways on 1st January 1948. By the 1950s the writing was really on the wall for steam.

D3 class 2365, the locomotive that reputedly brought down a German fighter at Lydd in 1942, is seen shortly after the incident. Despite what looks like terminal damage to its frames it was reportedly soon returned to traffic. (Original photographer unknown, courtesy Railway Magazine)

Greater prosperity saw the rise of the private motor car whilst a large surplus of war vehicles had seen an unprecedented increase in goods being transported by road throughout their journey, not just to and from the nearest railhead. If the railway was going to survive in any form it would have to modernise.

THE MODERNISATION PLAN

Nationally the British Railways Modernisation Plan of 1955 foresaw the eradication of steam and its replacement by mostly diesel traction by the early 1970s. In Kent electrification was on the menu, with all main lines (except Hastings) being electrified and re-signalled. The former LC&DR routes via North Kent to the Thanet coast and Dover would be first, followed by the routes via Ashford to the coast,

Platform lengthening for electrification (the live rail has already been laid) at Selling on 19th July 1958. L class 31768 stands in the station. (J.H. Ashton, R.C. Riley collection)

with completion set for 1962. Minor lines such as Paddock Wood–Strood and the Sheerness branch were included in the scheme. By the end of the 1950s BR was increasing the pressure to eliminate steam and nationally was ordering thousands of diesel locomotives of various designs from various manufacturers. In some areas steam was being eradicated in advance of electrification proposals. Diesels were therefore being introduced only to be rapidly superseded themselves, such was the desire of the modernisation programme to rid the railways of its perceived antiquated reputation. To an extent this was reflected in Kent. By the early 1960s diesel locomotives were replacing steam on the lines, which would be electrified only a couple of years or so later. Most of the locomotives themselves would remain in the county working freight or engineers' trains for the rest of their lives.

Normal steam working on the lines from London to Thanet ceased in June 1959. The main line from London to Folkestone and Dover was electrified in 1961, together with the secondary lines via Maidstone East and Canterbury West. Steam survived on miscellaneous workings until the start of 1962. Exactly what was the last steam passenger train on the main line in Kent is a matter of conjecture. On 25th February 1962 an enthusiasts' special made a farewell trip from London to Margate, returning

A Dover–Faversham train arrives at its destination. The locomotive is an ex-SE&CR D1 class, typical of the locomotives of venerable vintage that survived in Kent right up to the end of steam.
(Rev A.W.V. Mace, R.C. Riley collection)

The fate suffered by some steam locomotives before being finally broken up was conversion for use as stationary boilers. At Ramsgate on 14th May 1960, D class 31501's days are numbered as the new carriage shed for electric trains rises behind it. (R.C. Riley)

A sad occasion as the photographer notes that these proud survivors are employed on their very last trip to Ashford to be broken up for their scrap metal content. Locomotives 31749 and 31067 have been entrusted with two vans and are passing Knockholt on their last journey on 4th November 1961. (S.C. Nash, R.C. Riley collection)

The last day of services on the Hawkhurst branch, 10th June 1961. C class 31588 arrives at Cranbrook with the 4.25 pm from Paddock Wood, which has been strengthened to five coaches to cope with railway enthusiasts who have come for a final trip over the line. (R.C. Riley)

CRANBROOK

via a journey down the New Romney branch from Ashford and Appledore. A few locomotives were retained as stationary boilers at depots whilst Ashford Works hung onto a pair of 'USA' tank locomotives for shunting for as long as possible after steam ceased elsewhere in the county. It is probable that one of the pair brought the curtain down on steam in Kent in 1964, only a short distance away from where it had been raised by *Invicta* 134 years previously. Towards the end of steam there were still some wonderful Victorian locomotives in use. Most of them were broken up for their valuable scrap metal content at Ashford. Larger, more modern express locomotives built in the 1940s were transferred elsewhere in the Southern Region where steam lasted until 1967.

By the 1960s the steam locomotive was much maligned and was missed by few. Electrification had brought a quantum leap in the speed, efficiency and regularity of rail travel throughout the county. That is, of course, for those areas that still retained

Some of the locomotives introduced as part of the Modernisation Plan are still going strong in the second decade of the 21st century. A class 73 electro-diesel, one of the class introduced to eliminate steam in Kent, passes a distinctive 135 year old South Eastern Railway waiting shelter at Knockholt in February 2009. Snow, ice and electricity do not mix. Whilst steam would have battled on, this locomotive is employed on de-icing duties in an attempt to keep the third rail clear for steam's electric replacements. (Author)

Many of Kent's closed branch lines just returned to nature. Frittenden Road station on the old Kent & East Sussex Railway is seen 30 years after closure. (Author)

their railway. Lines to Hawkhurst, Westerham, Tenterden, Hythe, New Romney and the direct route from Canterbury to Folkestone had simply been closed. Some under the aegis of the infamous Beeching report, others not. Two lines in the south of the county, from both Tonbridge and Ashford to Hastings across the border into Sussex, remained diesel worked. The Tonbridge–Hastings line required bespoke narrow profile rolling stock on account of restricted tunnel clearance, whilst BR was looking to close the Ashford–Hastings line in any event. As far as British Rail was concerned the line had been drawn underneath the age of steam. Apart from railway enthusiasts, a handful of railwaymen with a sense of tradition and a few other assorted sentimentalists, in the brave new world of the 1960s nobody else really cared.

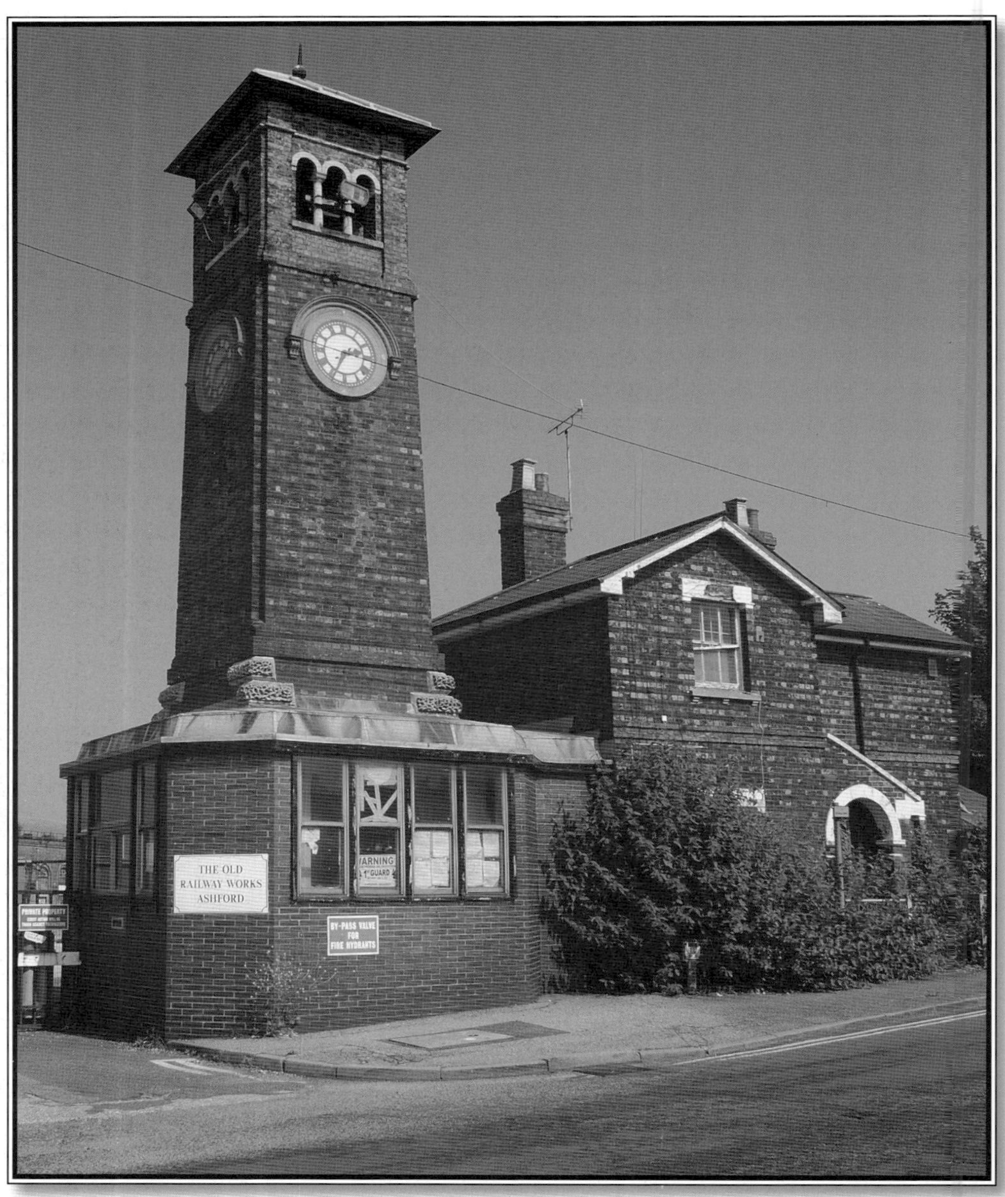

The entrance to Ashford Works sports an ornamental Italianate clock tower dating from 1855 together with a gate keeper's lodge. In 2010 they have seen better days. Behind them most of the mighty works is derelict. (Author)

The enormous water tower which served both Ashford works and the railway community of Newtown. Next door huddles the 'Alfred Arms' public house, built in 1866. Optimistically named after Watkin's son, the name Alfred Town found little local favour. The tower and the pub remain an enduring legacy of the SER's attempt to provide a 'model town' for their employees. (Author)

STEAM SURVIVORS

When the last fires of Kentish steam on the main line were being dropped in 1962, the steam heritage movement was yet to make any significant impact on the county. However, in one corner of Kent the steam railway lived on in much the same way that it had done for the previous 40 years.

THE WORLD'S SMALLEST PUBLIC RAILWAY

Promoted as a 'main line in miniature' the diminutive gauge of the Romney, Hythe & Dymchurch railway has led it to be dismissed by many people as an irrelevance. Yet since the 1920s it has been a unique and world famous part of the story of steam in Kent. In the late 1960s and early 1970s it was also the only steam passenger railway in Kent. It was born as a rich man's toy in the last days of the era when a cheque book could open any door provided it was large enough and the name on the front was influential enough. The story starts with a racing driver and a genuine aristocrat. Captain J.E.P. Howey, heir to a property fortune, and Count Louis Zborowski shared a passion for racing cars and drove competitively on the international circuit. Their attention turned to engineering in miniature and railways in particular. This was the era when the *Flying Scotsman* was the cutting edge of technology and out of a desire to reproduce the most up to date and fastest trains of the day in miniature, they looked for a suitably long and flat 'race track' on which they could perform. The flat seaboard of the Romney Marsh was ideal and in 1926 they set about creating their plaything between Hythe and New Romney, a complete 'toy' main line with double track, full signalling, locomotive works and stations. Tragedy struck when Zborowski was killed in a racing crash; thereafter Howey persisted alone.

The rich man's train set blossomed into the 'world's smallest public railway', curiously taken for granted locally yet possibly the most famous miniature railway on the globe. It soon set about providing a genuine service for locals and holidaymakers.

By 1928 it had been extended to Dungeness, a running line of 13½ miles, and it boasted a fleet of nine express locomotives. In the Second World War it served both its county and its country when one of its locomotives and some wagons were converted into an armoured train and carried an anti aircraft gun. It is rumoured this only happened to save the reputation of a War Ministry official who had misread a map and ordered an armoured train be provided on what he thought a strategically useful standard gauge line. After the war the battered line picked itself up and with high profile cinema duo Laurel and Hardy officiating at a relaunch, it was back in business. The railway's inherent problem was that, having been conceived as Captain Howey's plaything, its owner never really considered much about the railway's future beyond his lifetime. As his health failed, so did that of his railway, which by the 1970s was suffering from chronic under-investment. Following his death it went through many uncertain years and various owners. Closure and relocation were mooted but the line survives today on a more secure footing and is a famous and integral part of the landscape of a remote corner of the Kent coast.

The Romney Hythe & Dymchurch Railway's southern extremity at Dungeness. Locomotive No 6, Hercules, stands in the station on 4th June 2009. The vantage point of the top of the lighthouse shows the remoteness of the location. (Author)

On 15th April 1933 class O1 locomotive 1048 stands at Brasted station on the Dunton Green to Westerham branch, the line that was nearly saved for posterity. The site today is beneath the hard shoulder of the M25. (C.R. Gordon Stuart, courtesy Railway Magazine)

EARLY FAILURES

Today heritage railways and steam preservation are an accepted part of the leisure industry. It is a perception that has been a hard won battle over the last 40 years or so. The earliest attempts at establishing a living tribute to the legacy of steam in Kent foundered in a mire of official scepticism, ridicule and dark suggestions of a less than even playing field. The 5½ mile branch line from Dunton Green to Westerham in the north-west corner of the county had everything that a self contained heritage railway could wish for – a complete branch line with a main line junction at one end, to a terminus at the other serving a fair sized town, with plenty of sidings and space for rolling stock. The stations were all of traditional design, virtually unaltered since opening in 1881, with the intermediate one at Brasted being a wonderful rural gem. It was all less than 20 miles from Central London as well. When British Railways closed it in October 1961 a preservation society, with an eye on the success of the Bluebell Railway across the border in Sussex, swung into action. Leases were taken out on the stations, and a steam locomotive – the last of the H class tanks synonymous with the branch – was bought, with a C class of similar vintage promised. Carriages were purchased and in November 1963 terms of sale were agreed with BR. Only then did it become apparent that Kent County Council was interested in the railway land for road improvement schemes.

There had been dark rumours that the entire case for closure had been influenced by a desire to build what later became the M25 along the course of the line, but this was categorically denied by the Transport Ministry. A month after the terms of sale were agreed, the council raised the spectre of compulsory purchase. BR then broke off negotiations and sold the railway to the council instead. The council offered to lease the line back to the railway's supporters on an annual basis but required a new bridge to be built across it for the Sevenoaks by-pass (now part of the A21). A sum was quoted for the bridge and then without warning, when the railway's supporters were given a month's notice to find the funds, the quoted cost was inexplicably doubled. Unsurprisingly it was an impossible task. There was no bridge and the railway was severed to build the road. By the early 1980s much of the course of the line was indeed obliterated by the building of the M25, despite earlier protestations to the contrary.

The first active location for preserved standard gauge steam in Kent was the 'South Eastern Steam Centre', based at the former Ashford shed. During an open day in 1975 Hawthorn Leslie 0-4-0 saddle tank Singapore shuttles along one of the demonstration lines. The centre closed the following year. (Author)

Westerham would have been an outstanding steam heritage railway, so close to London, serving the town's tourist attractions and being a self contained and easy-to-operate line in its own right. It was doomed to failure by the road builders. Yet had BR sold the line to its supporters, and had the threat of compulsory purchase not been implemented, the road builders would probably had the last laugh. It is highly likely that the M25 motorway would still have been built right next to it in order to minimise the adverse effect of bisecting agricultural land. A six-lane motorway abutting a steam railway for most of its length would have robbed it of its soul.

Meanwhile in 1969 there was welcome progress on the narrow gauge front. The paper manufacturer Bowater's, who operated an extensive 2ft 6in gauge system from their mill at Sittingbourne to Ridham Dock on the Swale, decided to close their railway and turn transport over to road operation. Commendably they donated half the line plus a large selection of locomotives and rolling stock to the Locomotive Club of Great Britain. The line reopened in 1970 as the Sittingbourne & Kemsey Light Railway.

The next attempt at a standard gauge steam heritage site did get off the ground but ultimately fared no better. At the end of steam the very large depot at Ashford was rented to house the last remaining Victorian class O1 locomotive 31065, which had been bought for preservation. It was opened to the public as the 'South Eastern Steam Centre'. It soon boasted an impressive stock of steam locomotives owned by a whole host of individuals and societies. This included 'Merchant Navy' 35028 *Clan Line* and the H and C classes intended for Westerham. Regular steaming days were held both in the depot yard and along a quarter mile stretch of line, which included a platform built of old sleepers. The operation emulated a similar arrangement at Carnforth in Lancashire. Whereas the Carnforth operation was bolstered by the ability to attract visitors to steam hauled specials on the main line, the Ashford site was hemmed in by the electrified third rail on which steam was banned. Tempted by the chance to run locomotives either on the main line in other parts of the country or on preserved lines where they could stretch their legs further than the confines of the steam centre, owners started to take their locomotives away. As time moved on, more owners deserted the site and the operation withered. In August 1976 bailiffs took possession of the site following a court order for alleged non-payment of rent. Rolling stock owned by individuals and societies was moved out, but items seized by the bailiffs remained on site until the early 1980s. Thereafter, in an unprecedented move, authority was given for scrap merchants to cut up historic items of stock to realise their scrap metal value. Whilst 31065 survived (having been removed and split into constituent parts, scattered as far afield as Cambridgeshire) the sole surviving double deck trailer carriage built for the United Kingdom was torched.

On the Spa Valley Railway, Kent's latest steam heritage railway, ex-GWR Pannier tank 7715, passes through the Wealden woods near High Rocks on 2nd May 2009. (Author)

Final success

A standard gauge preserved railway was finally established when enthusiasts won a hard fought battle to revive Colonel Stephens' old Kent & East Sussex Railway. Its charm as a light railway spawned a determined campaign to restore it as a heritage line. It ran up against the same arguments that had thwarted Westerham. In this case, the government would not countenance the possibility of level crossings holding up traffic on A roads earmarked for eventual improvement. A proportion of Westerham supporters had thrown their lot in with the K&ESR after having seen their scheme defeated. Mindful of that defeat, the K&ESR abandoned its aspirations to reopen the section between Bodiam and Robertsbridge where the contentious crossings were located. It was not until 1974 that the first standard gauge public train ran on a preserved railway in Kent, when the section from Tenterden to Rolvenden was reopened. It is now one of the county's most popular tourist attractions and links Tenterden with Bodiam and its famous National Trust castle.

The next stage of the steam revival was the reopening of the remains of the East

A quiet moment on the Kent & East Sussex Railway. Terrier Sutton stands in the yard at Tenterden Town station. The Terrier class tank locomotives have always been associated with the railway, and two examples are based there in preservation. (Author)

The yard at Rolvenden shed on the restored Kent & East Sussex Railway harbours a fine selection of locomotives. In the foreground is one of the line's original machines – No 3 Bodiam. (Author)

Kent Railway between Shepherdswell and Eythorne. When reopened, this heritage line featured steam traction in its early days, but has latterly relied on diesel and uniquely battery electric operation, using restored Southern Region multiple units.

A group of enthusiasts formed the North Downs Steam Railway and spent many years in the 1980s and 1990s seeking a permanent base for their working locomotives and rolling stock. They led a nomadic existence operating at various times at Rochester, Higham, Chatham Dockyard and latterly at a green field site at Stone Lodge near Dartford. Various issues, not least vandalism and a perceived lack of support from the local authority, led them to give up their operation at Stone Lodge and transfer most of their assets to the embryonic Spa Valley Railway at Tunbridge Wells in 1996. The Spa Valley, running from Tunbridge Wells across the border to Eridge in Sussex, is the county's most recent steam railway. Although a relative newcomer, it does boast two unique features for a heritage railway in the South East. Firstly its locomotives are kept in a genuine Victorian locomotive shed. In this case an example built by the London, Brighton & South Coast Railway at Tunbridge Wells West in 1891. Although the Brighton company did not feature much in the history of railways in Kent it made sure it had a foothold in the lucrative Tunbridge Wells market. Its West station in the town was something of an outpost of the company but it did have the effect of defending its territory from the marauding SER, hungry for late 19th-century expansion. At its other end the Spa Valley enjoys the unique privilege of sharing the double track national network line for a mile into Eridge station, which it shares with national operator Southern.

There is one heritage site in Kent where the operation of steam remains timeless and unchanged from the 'golden age' – where a locomotive still works at the same place as it has done so for over 60 years and with the same rolling stock. Curiously, although famous itself, it is not well known for the operation of steam locomotives. It is Chatham Dockyard. Standard gauge came to the dockyard relatively late, in 1877, and gradually replaced an earlier narrow gauge system. It developed into a sprawling network serving over 350 acres. After the docks were closed in 1984 the site was divided into two; the larger half was sold for redevelopment whilst the smaller, more historic part with significant Georgian and Victorian infrastructure was preserved. Unfortunately the railway's locomotive shed was in the former part, but there was still plenty of running line in the retained part, to which the surviving locomotives and stock migrated. The dock's internal wagon pool was a bonanza of ancient stock from a diverse selection of pre-grouping railway companies. An original Navy locomotive named *Ajax*, delivered in 1941, is the dockyard railway's star turn. The current running line passes such a rich variety of architecture that it would look improbable if recreated as a model railway. It starts adjacent to the great Victorian covered slipways, meanders past the permanent berths of two preserved warships and a submarine, through the Georgian part of the docks and finally ends up parallel to the River Medway. There are no fake passenger 'services' in the docks; demonstration freights are worked by the steam locomotives roughly one weekend a month. It really is a gem, but oddly enough such is the historical importance of the overall site that the survival of the working railway tends to get overlooked.

The heritage railway scene is now well established in Kent – although the popularity of a family day out on a steam railway would have undoubtedly confounded die-hard commuters of previous generations. Steam railways have proved adept in tapping into the huge leisure industry that blossomed roughly at the time following the demise of steam. The railways have also taken advantage of a generally increased enthusiasm for all things 'heritage'. The provision of visitor amenities has vastly improved. Themed events, especially galas, Thomas the Tank Engine weekends and Santa Specials at Christmas substantially boost the coffers of heritage lines. Indeed some railways rely on the income from such events when day to day running only just balances the books.

RETURNING STEAM TO THE MAIN LINE

By the late 1980s, whilst the heritage railways were establishing themselves, there was still a rigid ban on main line steam locomotives working on the national network in Kent. British Rail had allowed steam excursions to run in other parts of the country since 1972. In 1974 a trip from Basingstoke to Westbury had resulted in incidents of trespass and BR quite justifiably feared what might happen should such incidents recur in close proximity to the electrified third rail. Accordingly, for 15 years the only permitted movements of steam locomotives were if they were hauled by diesel or electric locomotives. Many locomotives visited BR depot open days in this fashion. As the 1980s drew to a close the ban softened to allow a few steam locomotives to run under their own power to and from such events under cover of darkness. Still many people eagerly awaited the day when steam would work again in daylight. When it did happen it caught nearly everyone by surprise.

On 8th September 1990 'Battle of Britain' class loco *257 Squadron* was to be rededicated at Folkestone Central as part of celebrations to mark the 50th anniversary of the Battle of Britain. It was brought by road from Swindon to Ashford where it was to be hauled by rail to Folkestone Central. On the appointed day it was duly hauled from Ashford but only as far as Folkestone West, where to most people's surprise the class 73 electro-diesel on the front uncoupled and set off ahead of the steam locomotive. A short while later *257 Squadron* moved off under its own steam and followed into Folkestone Central. Although the distance was only a few hundred yards, the whistle screaming out over the rooftops of Folkestone announced that the main line steam ban was now well and truly over.

Steam's triumphant return to the main line. On 8th September 1990 'Battle of Britain' class locomotive 34072 257 Squadron steams into Folkestone Central. (Author)

Thereafter steam incrementally gained further footholds on the main line. The following year, to mark a local festival, steam returned to the now closed Folkestone Harbour branch. 'West Country' class *Taw Valley* and BR standard tank 80080 took centre stage in a highly popular weekend of shuttles up and down the branch. A year after that, 1992 marked the 150th anniversary of the railway reaching Ashford. There were steam excursions on the unelectrified line from Ashford to Hastings. On the evening of Sunday 7th June it was necessary to return the coaching stock to London and the train was run as a passenger working. The booking form stated 'Surprise motive power – not steam'. Few people were fooled and it was *Taw Valley* (again) bearing the 'Man of Kent' headboard that carried passengers by steam on the Kentish main line (as opposed to a branch or secondary line) for the first time in 30 years.

The ultimate reincarnation was the 'Golden Arrow'. Various steam hauled trains from London to the coast ran in the mid 1990s with the famous headboard and flags but with ordinary coaching stock. It was only when steam was matched with the luxury Venice Simplon Orient Express Pullman coaches that the spectacle – or

A classic recreation of Kentish main line steam. 'King Arthur' class locomotive 30777 Sir Lamie. passes the semaphore signals, manual level crossing gates and SER signal box at Chartham working a Victoria–Canterbury excursion on 6th November 1994. (Author)

was it a mirage? – was complete. With an eye on the commercial attractions of steam traction, the VSOE now runs several steam hauled trips around Kent each year where passengers can be pampered in the luxury surroundings and with all the trappings of the elite passenger in the age of steam.

OTHER REMINDERS

Aside from preserved steam locomotives and heritage lines there are a whole host of reminders of the age of steam still in everyday use on the national network. The modern railway is an industry constantly constrained by the infrastructure of the 19th century. Many station buildings in Kent are original structures; the oldest, which is one of the last surviving original SER wooden buildings, is located at Pluckley, incidentally a village reputed to be the most haunted in England. Other wooden structures in original or near original condition are rare. Bexley and Hildenborough are two of the best preserved, whilst the building at Eden Park on the Hayes branch has been restored with UPVC boards in place of the wooden clapboard. Lyminge

The recreation of the 'Golden Arrow'. 'Merchant Navy' class 35028 Clan Line, complete with headboard and flags, is paired with the Venice Simplon Orient Express Pullmans and is seen approaching Swanley on 15th November 2008. The obelisk on the right is a Victorian coal post, erected to show the location where extra taxes on coal being transported into London would become due. (Author)

on the closed Elham Valley Line from Canterbury to Ashford now serves as a public library. The matching signal boxes are in even shorter supply – only Cuxton, Snodland and Chartham survive. In contrast, nearly all of the brick or stone built Gothic, Tudor and Italianate examples survive. Wye, Cuxton, Aylesford, Wateringbury, Ham

South Eastern Railway infrastructure that survived into the 21st century. East Farleigh station between Paddock Wood and Maidstone West still retains its traditional features. The wooden building and signal box survive although the semaphore signals and level crossing gates have since been replaced. (Author)

Street and Appledore are still wonderful examples of the thought and craftsmanship that went into the design of Victorian country stations. At the time of writing, the buildings at Wye and Ham Street are still staffed and their ticket offices are still in use. Others, such as Cuxton, are empty whilst Aylesford is converted to an Indian restaurant.

A large proportion of the former LC&DR simple brick-built villa buildings survive. Most of the smaller stations between Swanley and Dover remain, with their distinctive incorporated stationmaster's houses. Some of the best survivors in the county are those between Swanley and Ashford, the distinctive 1880s structures east of Maidstone being particularly noteworthy. Healthy passenger use has ensured their survival and most are still staffed. Within a short distance from the capital, it is still possible to find immaculate waiting rooms and ticket halls with magazines put out to read and sometimes second-hand books for sale via honesty boxes. Even the odd flower arrangement can appear – an echo of the more civilised age of travel. As well as the station buildings, there are still a variety of other structures, such as waiting shelters and goods warehouses, dotted around the county, some significantly altered yet others surprisingly unchanged since the days of steam.

But the legacy of Watkin and Forbes and their bitter rivalry (see Chapter 1) still exerts itself on the social fabric of Kent in subtle ways. The 21st-century passenger has his daily life governed by the idiosyncrasies of the rivals' machinations of 150 years previously. If you want to set off on a trip to the seaside by train today, the resort you go to will depend upon which rival was promoting the railway through your town or village a century and a half ago. If it was Forbes, you will be off to Margate. If it was Watkin, it will be Hastings or Folkestone.

Appledore, an example of one of the well proportioned Italianate country stations, still remains, albeit unstaffed, on the Ashford–Hastings line. (Author)

The standard South Eastern railway design clapboard signal box. This well proportioned example is at Snodland, one of only three such buildings to survive into the 21st century. The unusual extension to the right (probably ideal for tomato growing!) was added later and may have once held a large wheel to operate the adjacent level crossing. (Author)

Similarly, some tiny communities enjoy an easy commute to London. Villages such as Marden and Headcorn enjoy a fairly rapid journey to the capital because their communities happened to be on the most economical route to build the railway to bring mail and passengers from the farthest corner of the British Empire. Larger towns such as nearby Cranbrook and Tenterden weren't, their railways withered and so in the 21st century they are not so attractive to commuters; the make-up of their population is therefore subtly different.

Across the face of the county, all the major engineering works, the tunnels and viaducts, are still those projected and built by those Victorian promoters. Most are taken for granted by those who pass them, with any historical significance lost in the hurry of the journey. It is particularly fitting to end the story where it began. Almost unknown and hidden, yet passed by thousands of people each day, are two reminders of the railway where the history of steam in Kent began. The London & Greenwich Railway's viaduct on the approach to London Bridge has now been widened from the original two tracks to thirteen in places. Yet, at its core, the original viaduct survives. The L&G in 1835 decided that its line would cross two

The heavy engineering of the last few miles of the South Eastern Railway's coastal line to Dover has left a legacy of one of the most scenic stretches of railway in the country. The portals of Shakespeare Cliff Tunnel's twin bores, once inspected by the Duke of Wellington, have become a distinctive part of the coastal landscape. Victorian physicians claimed the body would be asphyxiated by travelling at speeds of 30mph. What would they have made of the 140mph 'Javelin' trains?
(Katie Staines)

of the few existing streets by way of more impressive bridges than an ordinary arch. Accordingly, it faced the arches with ornamental stone and the tracks above were supported by classically finished iron columns. With the railway on either side expanded, their classical lines have been obscured by the later additions, but to this day the columns survive as listed structures. The effect is a latter day industrial version of the Renaissance Italian fashion of building a church around the supporting columns of a pre-existing ancient Greek or Roman temple. Its significance is totally lost or unknown to so many thousands of people who see or use it every day, yet it is part of the oldest remaining legacy of the age of steam in Kent and that desire to link London with the Continent and Empire of the 1830s.

The columns of the original Abbey Street bridge, built in 1835 by the London & Greenwich Railway, still serve their original purpose to this day. When this photograph was taken they had been holding up the railway for 175 years. (Author)

Bibliography

Armstrong Alan (Ed) *The Economy of Kent 1640–1914* Boydell Press/KCC
Bignell, Alan *Hopping down in Kent* Hale
Catt, A.R. *The East Kent Railway* Oakwood Press
Draper, Joyce *Historical Insights into Kent* Memoir Club
Ellis, Peter *The 150th Anniversary of the Opening of the Canterbury & Whitstable* British Rail
Esau, Mike & Siviour, Gerald *Kent Coast Heyday* Ian Allan
Garrett, S.R. *The Kent and East Sussex Railway* Oakwood Press
Gould, David *The Westerham Valley Railway* Oakwood Press
Gray, Adrian *The London, Chatham and Dover Railway* Meresborough Books
Gray, Adrian *The South Eastern and Chatham Railway* Middleton Press
Gray, Adrian *The South Eastern Railway* Middleton Press
Harding, Peter *The Hawkhurst Branch Line* Peter Harding
Harding, Peter *The New Romney Branch* Peter Harding
Hart, Brian *The Hundred of Hoo Railway* Wild Swan
Hylton, Stuart *Kent and Sussex 1940* Pen and Sword
Jessup, Frank *A History of Kent* Phillimore
Minns, John *Southern Country Stations, the SE&CR* Ian Allan
Snell, J.B. *One Man's Railway* David & Charles
South Eastern Steam Centre Trust *Illustrated Catalogue* SE Steam Centre
Staines, David *The Spa Valley Railway* Halsgrove
Thomas, R.H.G. *London's First Railway, the London & Greenwich* Batsford
White, H.P. *A Regional History of the Railways of Great Britain, Vol 2,* David & Charles
Wragg, David *Southern Railway Handbook 1923–1947* Sutton
Wright, Christopher *Kent Through the Years* Batsford

Index

Q

Queenborough 23, 24, 55–56

R

Railway Children, The 85, 87–88
Rainham 77
Ramsgate 24, 32–35, 58, 60, 72, 75, 97
Redhill 19, 24, 69
Richborough 13, 32, 72, 73
Ridham Dock 108
Robertsbridge 26, 27, 109
Rochester 21, 91, 111
Rolvenden 25, 27, 109, 110
Romney, Hythe & Dymchurch Railway 104–105
Romney Marsh 24, 57, 72, 77, 104
Rosherville 23
Rotherhithe 14, 61
Rother Valley Railway 27
Round Down Cliff 19, 30

S

St Mary Cray 22
Sandgate 28
Sandling 28, 48, 52
Park 31
Sandwich 32
Selling 95
Sevenoaks 24, 39, 44, 55, 57, 107
Tunnel 30
Shakespeare Cliff Tunnel 46, 120
Sheerness 23, 56, 96

Shepherdswell 50, 72, 73, 111
Sheppey, Isle of 15, 55
Shooters Hill and Eltham Park station 43
Shorncliffe 57, 78
Shortlands 22
Sidcup 42, 79
Sittingbourne 21, 108
Sittingbourne & Kemsley Light Railway 108
Snodland 115, 118
Snowdown colliery 60, 72, 73
South Eastern & Chatham Railway (SE&CR) 20, 24, 27, 38, 44, 96
South Eastern Railway (SER) 9, 19, 20, 21, 22–24, 32, 36, 46, 47 *seq*, 55, 56, 57, 58–59, 60, 63, 68 *seq*, 79 *seq*, 84 *seq*, 94, 100, 103, 111, 114, 116, 117, 120
South Eastern Steam Centre 107, 108
Southern Railway (SR) 9, 26, 27, 35, 36, 38, 39, 52, 57, 71, 90, 91, 94
Spa Valley Railway 9, 67, 109, 111
Staplehurst 46
Stephens, Col Holman F. 24–28, 72–73, 109
Stephenson, George 13
Stewarts Lane 54, 75
Stone Lodge 111
Strood 21, 22, 24, 96
Swanley 115, 116

T

Telford, Thomas 19
Tenterden 24, 27, 101, 109, 110, 119
'Thanet Belle' 58
Tilmanstone colliery 72, 73
Tonbridge 12, 20, 24, 26, 27, 32, 44, 64, 77, 78, 79, 80, 90, 101
Tunbridge Wells 20, 32, 78, 111
West 9, 77, 78, 87, 111
Tyler Hill Tunnel 70

V

Victoria, Queen 56
Victoria station 22, 42, 52–53, 56

W

Wadhurst 78
Walmer Castle 46
Warehorne 77
Wateringbury 67, 115
Watkin, Edward 22, 23–24, 26, 57, 87, 117
Wellington, Duke of 46
Westerham 32, 101, 106–108, 109
Westgate-on-Sea 33, 59
Whitstable 13 *seq*, 70
Woolwich 42, 63
Wye 115–116

Z

Zborowski, Count Louis 104

Other Kent titles from Countryside Books include:

www.countrysidebooks.co.uk